EDUCATION IN AMERICA

Quality vs. Cost

Timely Reports to Keep
Journalists, Scholars and the Public
Abreast of Developing Issues, Events and Trends

Editorial Research Reports
Published by Congressional Quarterly Inc.
1414 22nd Street, N.W.
Washington, D.C. 20037

About the Cover

The cover was designed by Steve Magnuson under the direction of Art Director Richard Pottern.

Editor, Hoyt Gimlin
Managing Editor, Sandra Stencel
Editorial Assistants, Claire Tury, Joseph Kessler
Production Manager, I. D. Fuller
Assistant Production Manager, Maceo Mayo

Library of Congress Cataloging in Publication Data
Main entry under title:

Editorial research reports on education in America, quality vs. cost.

Bibliography: p.
Includes index.
1. Public school — United States — Cost effectiveness. 2. Education — United States — Cost effectiveness. I. Congressional Quarterly, inc.
LA217.E34   370′.973   81-12621
ISBN 0-87187-212-9   AACR2

Contents

Foreword

"That there is something ailing the public schools has become a dreary commonplace," pollster George Gallup wrote. "But just how widespread this idea is, just how deeply engraved it is in the public's mind," he added, is shown most starkly in national opinion surveys. He was commenting on last year's Gallup Poll of a cross-section of Americans in which only 10 percent gave their local schools an A for quality. In this year's poll, the figure slipped to 9 percent, slightly better than the low point of 8 percent in 1979 but only half as good as in 1974, the year these annual surveys were first conducted for Phi Delta Kappa, the professional education organization.

In that time span the number of people who had no opinion about the quality of local schools dropped from 20 to 10 percent. Dr. Wilmer Bugher, associate executive secretary of Phi Delta Kappa, considers this "a significant shift in awareness" and attributes it to growing dissatisfaction with public education. This thought is also borne out in the responses to a question in the 1981 poll asking if the increased number of non-public schools is "good" or "bad." Forty-nine percent said good, while 30 percent said bad.

The private school boom and the public's flirtation with tax support for private schooling through tuition tax credits are the focus of two Reports among those in this book examining current education issues. Public funds for private education, once almost exclusively a "parochiaid" question, finds new appeal in the non-Catholic middle class as disenchantment with public education rises.

This disenchantment extends also to business, which — as another Report portrays — is spending billions every year to provide workers with some of the fundamentals they did not learn in the classroom. Competency tests reflect official acknowledgement that high school graduates may enter the work place unequipped for jobs demanding basic reading and math skills. All the while that public schools are being accused of failing to educate children generally, they are under pressure to provide both for the handicapped and the gifted.

To many Americans the overriding question arising from these separate but related problems is whether the public schools ultimately can — indeed should — survive. Interestingly, the same kind of question is asked, for different reasons, about the future of many private colleges, especially the traditionally black colleges whose plight is described in this book.

Hoyt Gimlin
Editor

Washington, D.C.
September 1981

TUITION TAX CREDITS

by

Jean Rosenblatt and Hoyt Gimlin

**Aug. 14
1 9 8 1**

TUITION TAX CREDITS

W ITH President Reagan's election last November, 1981 seemed to be the year Congress would pass a law enabling taxpayers to deduct some of the cost of sending their children to private schools. A tuition tax credit bill won House approval and picked up 41 votes in the Senate in 1978, and the 1980 elections, bringing a Republican majority to the Senate, improved the political climate for passage in the new Congress.

The Republican Party's 1980 platform championed tuition tax credits as "a matter of fairness, especially for low-income families, most of whom would be free for the first time to choose for their children those schools which best correspond to their own cultural and moral values." And unlike President Carter who opposed tuition tax credits, President Reagan expressed his support for them. Sen. Bob Packwood, R-Ore., reintroducing a tuition tax credit bill he was cosponsoring for the third straight Congress with Sen. Daniel Patrick Moynihan, D-N.Y., said on Feb. 24: "With the wholehearted support of the Reagan administration, I expect the 97th Congress will see passage of this vital legislation."

To become effective in August 1982, it would provide a refundable federal income tax credit for half of the tuition, up to $250, paid by a taxpayer, spouse or dependent at any private elementary, secondary or vocational school or college that had a tax-exempt status with the Internal Revenue Service. A year later the maximum credit would rise to $500, and in 1984 it would extend to graduate students and half-time enrollees in colleges and vocational schools.

By the time Congress adjourned for its August recess, however, the outlook for passage in 1981 had grown exceedingly dim. The proposal came up at a time when the administration was busy cutting the federal budget, including direct aid for education, and income taxes. In addition to any other misgivings about tuition tax credits that individual members of Congress might have, they would find it awkward to vote for a program expected to cost the Treasury billions in lost revenues at the same time they were cutting appropriations and giving taxpayers general relief.

Soon after the Senate Subcommittee on Taxation and Debt Management held hearings on the bill, June 3-4, the administra-

3

tion asked that consideration be delayed until its tax-reduction legislation cleared Congress. The parent Finance Committee, in a move regarded as a tactical maneuver more than an expression of philosophy, voted not to send the tuition tax credit bill to the floor for a debate.

The tax-reduction legislation gained final passage on Aug. 4, leaving little time in the remaining session, which resumes Sept. 9, for as emotional an issue as tuition tax credits to be considered fully. It involves not only the right of parents to receive tax relief for sending their children to private schools, but also raises such fundamental questions as the future of public schools, and the separation of church and state.

Widening of Support Beyond 'Parochiaid'

Despite the diminished prospect for passage in 1981, tuition tax credit legislation is far from dead. Backing for the idea has broadened beyond the Catholic "parochiaid" issue of years past.[1] The debate today cuts across religious, political and racial lines, enlisting support from among both middle-class and low-income parents, white and black, who are unhappy with public education. Increasingly they have turned to private schools and, it is argued, more would like to do so if they could afford it.

Although Catholic-school enrollment has been slipping, it has been offset by gains in other private schools. Overall, the private school total has held steady for the past two years at about 5.1 million, accounting for about 11 percent of all students in America's primary and secondary schools. Enrollment in independent schools, those not affiliated with a church or synagogue, has been growing by about 2 percent a year. Among low-income and minority students, the enrollment increase has been about 10 percent a year, according to John C. Esty Jr., president of the National Association of Independent Schools. Public schools, on the other hand, have declined from 46.1 million students to 39.8 million during the past 20 years, the National Center for Education Statistics reports.

Statistics such as these provide arguments for both sides in the tuition tax credit fight. Proponents say they point up an increasing dissatisfaction with public education and the need for a tax-supported alternative. Opponents say the public schools were never in greater need of support and will be undermined if parents receive a tax incentive to put their children in private schools.

Support for tuition tax credits is based on the belief that they will enhance parental freedom of choice and reduce the finan-

---

[1] See "Catholic Schools," *E.R.R.*, 1964 Vol. II, pp. 561-579.

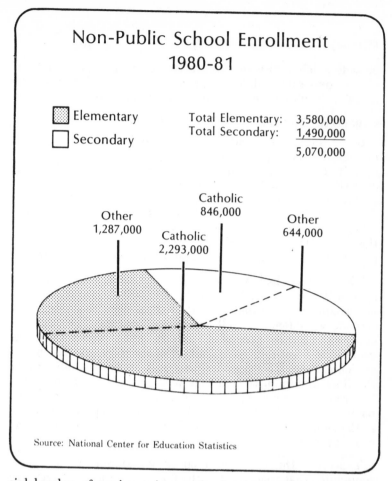

Non-Public School Enrollment
1980-81

▨ Elementary

☐ Secondary

Total Elementary: 3,580,000
Total Secondary: 1,490,000

5,070,000

Catholic
846,000

Other
1,287,000

Catholic
2,293,000

Other
644,000

Source: National Center for Education Statistics

cial burden of paying private school tuition. The Council for American Private Education, a coalition of 15 national organizations whose schools enroll about 85 percent of all private school students, casts the thought in these terms: "The constitutional right of parents to choose their child's school is being increasingly jeopardized by the increasing costs of private schools and of family existence."[2] The median tuition at the secondary level for the 894 member schools of the National Association of Independent Schools is $4,196 for day students and $6,159 for boarders. However, the range is vast, from $7,200 at Exeter, one of New England's prestigious preparatory schools, to $125 a month in the Chicago ghetto. Some parochial schools charge even less.

What private schools do for the public interest is at the heart of the dispute over tuition tax credits. Supporters say that private schools ensure pluralism in American education; offer competition and standards of comparison for public education;

[2] Testimony before the Senate Finance Subcommittee on Taxation and Debt Management, June 3, 1981.

provide a laboratory for innovative teaching ideas and techniques; and save public education money by educating one-tenth of the nation's elementary and secondary school students.

Organized Opposition by Teacher Groups

If the idea of tax credits has won new support, it also has mobilized strong opposition. This opposition is led by, or concentrated in, such groups as the American Federation of Teachers (AFL-CIO), the National Education Association, the League of Women Voters and the American Civil Liberties Union. These and 37 other school, civil rights, good-government and religious groups *(see listing, opposite),* under the umbrella of the National Coalition for Public Education, opened a campaign to defeat the 1981 legislation soon after it was introduced.

The coalition had been defunct since its vigorous lobbying against the 1978 bill. That year the Senate balked at passing the House-approved bill that provided tax relief for elementary and secondary students as well as college students. The 1981 bill applies to all three groups of students, but the push for it has been almost entirely on behalf of elementary and secondary students. Indeed, college administrators oppose the bill for fear the Reagan administration may attempt to substitute tuition tax credits for other types of student assistance.[3] Congressional passage of the Middle Income Student Assistance Act in 1978, at Carter's insistence, turned aside the colleges' support of tax credits that year.

This year the coalition focused its arguments on costs, contending that enactment of the bill would drain the Treasury of needed tax revenues at a time when financial resources are strained and the Reagan administration is busy cutting non-defense programs. The Treasury Department submitted the following tax loss estimates to the Senate Finance subcommittee:

	1982	1983	1984	1985	1986
	(in millions of dollars)				
Elementary and secondary	40	1,082	2,030	2,198	2,276
College	59	1,609	3,130	4,410	4,581
Total	99	2,691	5,160	6,608	6,857

The coalition insists that the figures might run far higher. "Once initiated," the American Federation of Teachers said in a

---

[3] Voicing opposition to the bill at the Senate Finance subcommittee hearing were spokesmen for the American Association of Community and Junior Colleges, made up of 1,231 community, junior and technical colleges; the American Council on Education, an organization of over 1,600 public and independent colleges and universities; and the National Association of Independent Colleges and Universities, with a membership of 850 institutions.

National Coalition for Public Education

The coalition lists the following major organizations as members:

American Alliance for Health, Physical Education, Recreation & Dance; American Association of Colleges for Teachers Education; American Association of School Administrators; American Civil Liberties Union; Americans for Democratic Action; American Ethical Union; American Federation of State, County & Municipal Employees; American Federation of Teachers; American Humanist Association; American Jewish Congress;

A. Philip Randolph Institute; Americans United for the Separation of Church and State; American Vocational Association; Baptist Joint Committee for Public Affairs; Board of Church & Society/United Methodist Church; Children's Defense Fund; Council for Educational Development and Research; Council of Chief State School Officers; Council of Great City Schools; Labor Council for Latin American Advancement;

League of Women Voters of the United States; Mexican American Legal Defense Educational Fund; National Association of Elementary School Principals; National Association for the Advancement of Colored People; National Association of School Psychologists; National Association of State Boards of Education; National Committee for Citizens in Education; National Congress of Parents and Teachers; National Council of Jewish Women; National Council of Senior Citizens;

National Education Association; National Public Education and Religious Liberty; National School Boards Association; National School Public Relations Association; National School Volunteer Program; National Urban League; New York City Board of Education; Student NEA; Union of American Hebrew Congregations; United Automobile, Aerospace and Agricultural Implement Workers of America; United States Student Association.

position paper, "tuition tax credits would provide an incentive for private schools to raise their tuitions and for parents of private school students to lobby for increased tax credits. If more parents decide to send their children to non-public schools and if the number of these schools increases, so will the pressure for larger tax credits."

The argument that tuition tax credits will undermine financial support for public schools is particularly disturbing to public educators in light of President Reagan's cuts in education funding this year. Less than $200 of the current average per pupil expenditure comes from federal sources. So a $500 subsidy for a child in a private school would be over twice the amount received by a public school student. In addition, opponents believe that the cost of tuition credits would force Congress to make up the tax losses from existing public education programs.

A big fear among educators is the loss in state aid — and the subsequent loss of jobs for teachers — that would accompany further declines in public school enrollments. The AFT has estimated that a 25 percent increase in private school enrollment would throw about 66,000 public school teachers out of work. A *Newsweek* poll conducted by the Gallup organization last spring found that 23 percent of the parents surveyed said they would probably enroll their children in private schools if tuition tax credits became available. However, E. G. West, writing for the Heritage Foundation, a conservative-oriented research organization in Washington, D.C., said that on the basis of past responsiveness of private school enrollments to tuition reductions the figure was likely to be no more than 3 percent.[4]

At the Senate subcommittee hearings, West denied that tax credits would undermine public education. He said that with "each batch of [student] transfers there will be significant gains to ... taxpayers ... because private schooling costs [per student] are about one-half of those in public schools. At a cost of $500 foregone federal tax revenue, state and local governments would save more than an equal amount for each student transferring, since it will no longer be necessary to educate him at public cost in the usual way."

While supporters of tuition tax credits claim that low-income families would benefit, opponents insist that the credits are essentially subsidies for families who need help the least. According to an NEA position paper: "The choice provided by this tax break will not be available to the majority of public school parents, because the actual cost of private school tuition is prohibitive to many middle- and lower-income parents. The real tax break will be only for those middle- and upper-income parents who can afford to pay the balance of a school's tuition not subsidized by the tax credits." In addition, the NEA said, all taxpayers wuld be paying for the support of private schools, even if their children were not enrolled in them.

Parents of private school children use the same argument in reverse. By paying taxes, they say, they are supporting public schools their children do not use. AFT President Albert Shanker retorts: "If I don't like the drinking water, I can't ask you to pay for my Perrier. . . . We do have choices, but it seems to me that there's no obligation on the part of the taxpayer to pay for those private choices."[5]

The NEA argues that tuition tax credits would create an educational caste system with the "haves" in private schools and the "have nots" in public schools. Private schools, unlike their public counterparts, are not mandated to accept children who are handicapped, pose discipline problems, or are difficult

---

[4] E. G. West, "The Economics of Education Tax Credits," booklet published by the Heritage Foundation, 1981. West is professor of economics at Carleton University, Ottawa, Canada, and adjunct scholar at the Heritage Foundation.

[5] Remarks made at a news conference in Washington conducted June 1, 1981, by the National Coalition for Public Education.

to teach. Private schools can afford to be selective, while public schools must accept all students. "It is not inconceivable," the NEA said, "that the contrast between the elite private schools and the disadvantaged public schools will increasingly amount to a separate and unequal education system in the United States."[6]

Church-State Issue; Religious Divisions

Strong opposition to tuition tax credits is based on the fact that 80 to 90 percent of the non-public school students attend church-affiliated schools. Opponents tend to see tax credits as federal support of religious education in violation of the First Amendment's freedom-of-religion ("establishment") clause. It states: "Congress shall make no law respecting an establishment of religion, or prohibiting the free exercise thereof." Proponents contend that this view is a misreading of the Constitution's intent.

The two men most responsible for the inclusion of that clause, Thomas Jefferson and James Madison, interpreted it absolutely: that it prohibited a presidential proclamation of Thanksgiving or a tax exemption for churches. The Supreme Court, however, has never adopted the absolutist position. In its first decision on the clause, in 1899, the court upheld a federal construction grant to a Catholic hospital, saying that the hospital's purpose was secular and that it did not discriminate among its patients on the basis of religion.[7]

Since that decision, only two areas of national life have raised significant establishment-clause questions — public schools and taxes. The court has sustained the practice of exempting churches from taxes on the ground that to tax them would entangle the government excessively with religion. The court, however, has adopted what it describes as a "benevolent neutrality" toward government financial aid for parochial schools. If the aid is secular in purpose and effect, and does not entangle the government excessively in its administration, it is permissible even if it indirectly benefits church schools.[8]

The first case challenging state aid — free textbooks — to a church-related school reached the court in 1930. Adopting the "child benefit" theory, it held that free textbooks provided by Louisiana taxpayers for parochial schools were intended to further the education of all children and not to benefit church schools. Then in 1947 the court elaborated on this reasoning. By a 5-4 vote, it upheld a New Jersey law to repay parents the cost

---

[6] "NEA Position Paper on Tuition Tax Credits," January 1981, p. 4.
[7] *Bradfield v. Roberts*, 210 U.S. 50 (1899).
[8] See "Establishment of Religion," chapter in Congressional Quarterly's *Guide to the Supreme Court* (1979), pp. 461-471.

of sending their children to school, public or parochial, on public transportation. A much-quoted majority opinion by the late Justice Hugo L. Black said the First Amendment "requires the state to be a neutral in its relations with groups of religious believers and non-believers; it does not require the state to be an adversary."[9]

Over the next 20 years the Supreme Court decided a series of school prayer cases, ruling that the establishment clause did not permit public schools to use prayers and Bible readings because such exercises were sectarian and their primary effect was to advance religion. In 1971 the court incorporated these criteria as a test of constitutionality for any plan to aid a parochial school.[10] The law promoting such a plan must have a secular purpose and a primary effect that neither advances nor inhibits religion and must not foster "an excessive government entanglement with religion." Using this three-part test the court ruled unconstitutional in 1973 a New York plan for tuition reimbursement and credits similar to the 1981 federal proposal. Writing for the court, Justice Lewis F. Powell Jr. said "the effect of the aid is unmistakably to provide financial support for non-public, sectarian institutions."[11]

An editorial in the March 1981 issue of *Church and State,* a magazine published by Americans United for Separation of Church and State, said that the very process of trying to pass tuition tax credits legislation would involve excessive entanglement between religion and government, since it is church groups that are lobbying for legislation.[12] But while Catholic-school interests are lobbying for federal parochiaid, many supporters of the newer Protestant schools are holding back, mostly out of fear of unwelcome federal control on hiring and admissions that might accompany federal money.

Indeed, religious groups are split on tuition tax credits. Siding with the Catholic Church are the Missouri Synod of the Lutheran Church, which represents about a third of the Lutherans in the United States, the Christian Reformed Church and individual Baptists identified with the Moral Majority. Orthodox Jewish groups are largely in favor of tuition tax credits, although Conservative and Reform groups tend to oppose the idea. Also opposing it are the largest body of Baptists, the Southern Baptist Convention, and the Unitarian Universalist Association and Seventh-day Adventists. The fact that several other Protestant churches have taken no formal position is generally assumed to be a sign of opposition.

---

[9] *Everson v. Board of Education,* 330 U.S. 1. The previous case was *Cochran v. Louisiana Board of Education,* 281 U.S. 370.
[10] *Lemon v. Kurtzman,* 403 U.S. 602 (1971).
[11] *Committee for Public Education and Religious Liberty v. Nyqist,* 413 U.S. 756 (1973).
[12] See "Tax Credit Parochiaid: The New Onslaught," p. 4.

The rocky constitutional history of indirect aid to parochial schools has been a deterrent to congressional action on tax credit proposals over the years. Proponents, including Senator Moynihan, obviously do not believe they are unconstitutional. "The final resolution of this question must be provided by the Supreme Court," he said upon introduction of the Moynihan-Packwood bill. "All one asks is the opportunity to put it before the court, something that can only happen if we stop interposing the constitutional question ahead of the public policy issue and proceed to enact a law that the court can examine."

Private vs. Public Education

WHAT ACCOUNTS for the increasing popularity of private education? White middle-class parents are being accused of taking their children out of the public schools to escape the poor, the black and handicapped. Many white families assert that their reasons for fleeing the public schools have more to do with quality education than desegregation.

Blacks as well as whites are leaving the public schools. The Council for American Private Education estimates that blacks and Hispanics now account for 17 percent of the students in Catholic schools and 13 percent of the students in Lutheran schools, the nation's second-largest group of church schools. Some experts say that as many as 40 percent of black middle-class families choose private education, proportionally more than white families in comparable economic circumstances.

The Rev. Andrew M. Greeley, a sociologist and Catholic priest, recently released a study showing that blacks and Hispanics from similar backgrounds perform better in Catholic schools than in public schools.[13] Greeley found that the differences were widest for blacks and Hispanics from the poorest and most educationally deprived families. "Something seems to be happening in the Catholic schools that is not happening in the public schools," Greeley said. "It leads me to conclude that the Catholic schools, which were set up to help poor immigrants, now do the same for minorities."[14]

The number of black private schools is also reported to be on the rise. Black educators estimated last year that in New York City there were nearly 100 of these private schools with an

---

[13] See Andrew M. Greeley, "Minority Students in Catholic Secondary Schools," Ford and Spencer Foundations, 1981.
[14] Quoted in "The Bright Flight," *Newsweek*, April 20, 1981, p. 68.

U.S. Catholic Schools

School year	Number of schools		Enrollment	
	Elementary	Secondary	Elementary	Secondary
1929-30	7,923	2,123	2,222,598	241,869
1949-50	8,589	2,189	2,560,815	505,572
Fall 1964	10,832	2,417	4,533,771*	1,066,748
1967-68	10,350	2,277	4,105,805	1,092,521*
1969-70	9,695	2,076	3,607,168	1,050,930
1970-71	9,370	1,980	3,355,478	1,008,088
1971-72	8,982	1,859	3,075,785	959,000
1972-73	8,761	1,743	2,871,000	919,000
1973-74	8,569	1,728	2,714,000	907,000
1974-75	8,437	1,690	2,602,000	902,000
1975-76	8,329	1,647	2,525,000	889,000
1976-77	8,265	1,617	2,483,000	882,000
1977-78	8,204	1,593	2,421,000	868,000
1978-79	8,159	1,564	2,365,000	853,000
1980-81	8,100	1,540	2,293,000	846,000

*Peak enrollment

Source: National Center for Education Statistics

enrollment of several thousand students. Moreover, black educators say that the majority of the children are from working-class families. Tuition ranges from about $450 to $2,000 a year at these schools.

What do private schools offer that attracts parents? First of all, they offer control. Administrators can select applicants according to academic standards they set themselves and require that students, once enrolled, meet those standards. Parents value the physically safe environment of many private schools. Perhaps most important to a growing number of parents is the moral instruction or emphasis on character and values that private schools offer.

This concern is not limited to schools being founded or backed by fundamentalist Protestant churches and churchgoers in the South, but it has been most evident there. Many "Christian academies" were established after local public schools became integrated, and typically they catered to white students only. Today the growth of fundamentalist private schools is closely related to the growth of the Moral Majority.

The number of these schools is not known — estimates run up to 10,000 — and they may be elaborate institutions or something scarcely more than a living room where a handful of kids are taught to read and write. Donald R. Howard, president of Accelerated Christian Education, which helps churches establish schools, says the average enrollment in 3,400 of these schools it has helped set up in recent years is about 75.

Denis Doyle, a resident fellow in education at the American Enterprise Institute, detects other trends that help explain the growing interest in private education. "Important shifts in family size, composition, and employment," Doyle wrote in the *Phi Delta Kappan* last year, "are having an impact on family taste in education."[15] More families in which husbands and wives work and the fact that couples are postponing childbearing and having fewer children means that families have more income available for expenses like private schooling. Americans also are highly motivated to obtain a good education for children. "Many middle-class parents who see education . . . as central to long-term income production . . . are willing to 'invest' in private schooling," he added. "In a middle-class country," he continued, "as the middle class goes so goes public policy. It should be no surprise, then, that private schools are beginning to move closer to the top of the nation's education agenda."

Rising Dissatisfaction With Public Schools

Although 75 percent of the nation's children graduate from high school, as opposed to the less than 60 percent three decades ago, cynicism about the quality of public education permeates inner cities and suburbs alike. While the much-publicized problems of public schools are very real, there is also a sense among some educators that they are under attack more than is warranted. "We are victims of our success," said Paul Salmon, executive director of the American Association of School Administrators. "We have a higher level now of education among our general population than we have ever had. The more educated people are, the less awe they hold educators in. . . . You can find examples in the educational system to support almost any generalization you want to make."[16]

In his first major address as secretary of education, Terrel H. Bell suggested that pessimism about the public schools was an inevitable part of the national mood. "When we lack confidence in ourselves, when we are troubled and when we are not prospering," he said, "it reflects in the nation's attitude, respect and support for schools."

Part of public schools' dilemma is what many see as federal interference in education. Busing is still controversial. Many parents have enrolled their children in private schools to avoid it and, even among families committed to integration, feelings about the value of busing are mixed. Administrators say they

---

[15] Denis P. Doyle, "Public Policy and Private Education," *Phi Delta Kappan*, September 1980, p. 16.
[16] National Coalition for Public Education news conference, June 1, 1981.

are overwhelmed by paperwork generated by efforts to direct federal aid to needy students, and teachers complain that federal regulations interfere with their ability to do their jobs.

For example, a law passed in 1975 providing for the education of all handicapped students in the least restrictive setting requires that handicapped children be placed in the same classroom as normal children, a practice known as mainstreaming.[17] This means that teachers — many of whom are ill-prepared to teach the handicapped — may spend a disproportionate amount of time with handicapped students at the expense of the others. Teachers must also acquire skills for dealing with the variety of handicaps, a field once the sole occupation of specialists.

In addition, a post-baby-boom decline in the number of school-age children has eroded enrollments, lowering school budgets already stretched thin by inflation. At the same time there has been a steady rise in enrollments of minorities in the suburbs, creating some of the same problems that in earlier years caused middle-class whites — then middle-class blacks — to flee.

The loudest and bitterest complaints about public schools concern discipline. Truancy, violence and drug and alcohol abuse, once aberrations, are now part of public-school life. In addition the Supreme Court ruling in 1969[18] that students do not "shed their constitutional rights ... at the schoolhouse gate" has made it difficult to suspend or expel students. While students enjoy their rights of citizenship, teachers struggle to maintain control in the classrooms and impose academic demands.

Frustration, a sense of helplessness, low pay and lack of job security has contributed to the recent phenomenon of teachers' "burnout." Many teachers are simply dropping out. When New York City faced bankruptcy in 1976, thousands of teachers were laid off, but only a quarter of them chose to return to their jobs when the city could afford to hire them back. A nationwide poll of teachers taken last year by the NEA showed that more than a third were dissatisfied with their jobs, and 41 percent regretted having become teachers.

J. Myron Atkins, dean of education at Stanford University, warns that a steep decline in the quality of students entering teacher training programs bodes ill for the future of public schools. He reported that verbal SAT (Scholastic Aptitude

---

[17] See "Mainstreaming: Handicapped Children in the Classroom," *E.R.R.*, 1981 Vol. II, pp. 533-535.
[18] *Tinker v. Des Moines Independent Community School District*, 393 U.S. 503.

Test) scores of high school seniors intending to teach had dropped to an average of 392 (SAT scores range from a low of 200 to a high of 800). Atkins contends that colleges and universities have lowered their standards to maintain enrollments in their education programs, which now attract only half as many students as they did in 1973.

The women's movement has opened up new careers for women for whom education used to be one of only a few options. "American public education owes much of its success to the exploitation of prominent women," said Lyn Gubser of the National Council for Accreditation of Teacher Education.[19] Low pay, poor job security, boredom, and a loss of faith in education also discourage bright young people from becoming teachers.

Controversy Over the Coleman Report

Fuel for the argument that private schools are superior to public schools has been provided by University of Chicago sociologist James Coleman. That seemed to be the conclusion he drew in a report, "Public and Private Schools," he was preparing for the National Center for Education Statistics, a division of the U.S. Department of Education. The study, based on data on 58,728 students in 1,015 public and private high schools, was the largest survey of non-public schools ever conducted by the federal government.

Coleman is known for his 1966 report on "Equality of Educational Opportunity," which was used by many to justify busing. He reported that poor blacks did better academically when they attended classes with a middle-class white majority. Twelve years after the report's publication, Coleman acknowledged that subsequent research had proven his earlier findings wrong and that some of his research methods had been inadequate.

University of Chicago photo
James Coleman

This report, too, came under attack and caused him to retreat from his initial assertion of private-school superiority. When a draft of the report was released last spring, it elicited widespread criticism from other researchers. Soon afterward, Coleman admitted that the data on which his finding had been based was flawed and, moreover, that his most significant conclusion had not been emphasized. In an interview with *The New York Times,* Coleman said his main finding was not that private schools were necessarily better but that effective private and public schools

[19] Quoted in "Teachers are in Trouble," *Newsweek,* April 27, 1981, p. 79.

15

shared certain characteristics, like high academic standards and an ordered environment. "Good public schools do just as well as those in the private sector, but if I were writing the report again I would focus more on how public policy can help schools in both sectors to be more effective."[20]

The federally funded National Assessment of Educational Progress, based in Denver, Colo., recently concluded from a study of the reading abilities of 100,000 children aged 9, 13 and 17 that private and public school children from similar family and economic backgrounds do about the same quality of work.[21] Another study, this one of private schools done by the Department of Education's National Institute of Education, said that "public schools must begin to look at those aspects of private schools that make people willing to pay for them." It suggested that "public schools could organize themselves along curricular and philosophic lines that parallel private schools."[22]

Advocates of tuition tax credits have used Coleman's findings to counter charges that private schools are racist and that tax credits would help white families avoid racial integration. Coleman, who favors tuition tax credits, observed that "the segregation of black and white students in U.S. schools is no greater and no less than it would be if there were no private schools."[23]

Government's Role in Education

PUBLIC FUNDS for private education, at issue in the tuition tax credits debate, bring up the larger question of the federal government's proper role in education. Traditionally, education has been primarily the function of state and local governments, and both supporters and opponents of tuition tax credits seem to like this arrangement. A Gallup Poll asked last year whether the federal, state or local government should have the greatest influence in deciding what is taught in the public schools. Only 9 percent of the respondents favored federal influence.[24]

While campaigning for the presidency, Ronald Reagan said of the new Department of Education: "I believe it is naive to think

[20] Quoted in *The New York Times*, June 3, 1981.
[21] See "Reading Achievement in Public and Private Schools: Is There a Difference?" National Assessment of Educational Progress, April 1981.
[22] Susan Abramowitz and others, "The Private High School Today," National Institute of Education, 1980.
[23] James Coleman, "Public and Private Schools," a report to the National Center for Education Statistics by the National Opinion Research Center, March 1981, p. xxv.
[24] Cited by George H. Gallup, "The 12th Annual Gallup Poll on the Public's Attitude Toward the Public Schools," *Phi Delta Kappan*, September 1980, p. 36.

that it is anything but a first step toward federalized education in the land."[25] However, the first person to become secretary of education, Carter-appointee Shirley M. Hufstedler, had a different view: "The real control of education is determined by where the money comes from, and the federal government supplies only 8 percent of the money for financing elementary and secondary education."[26]

Secretary of Education Terrel H. Bell, Hufstedler's successor, has recommended that the Department of Education be abolished and its functions handed over to a federal foundation of less-than-Cabinet rank. Such a move would be in line with Reagan's commitment to lessen the federal role of education and the 1980 Republican platform's call for the department demise. Bell sent an option paper to the White House listing at least four major ways to abolish the department. The administration wants to make a decision and send a reorganization proposal to Congress late this year.

The Reagan administration has pushed for a drastic retreat from federal regulation of education in another way also. This avenue of retreat is the consolidation of several categorical grant programs — those administered by the federal government and intended for special groups of people or programs — into two block grants. In proposing block grants, Reagan said they would give state and local officials more control over how federal education funds are spent in their communities, and would end burdensome federal regulation and paperwork that educators have long complained about.

But the Senate excluded the two largest education programs Reagan wanted in block grants: education for the handicapped and compensatory education of poor children.[27] Critics of block grants include many of the same groups that oppose tuition tax credits. They fear that without federal restrictions on how federal money is used, poor school districts will lose out and programs with the least political clout will not survive.

Bigger Federal Interest in Private Education

It can be argued that tuition tax credits are in step, or are way out of step, with the administration's philosophy of reducing federal influence in education. They are in step if one regards the support for private schools as being indirect, through the tax code. They are out of step if viewed as a federal decision to

---

[25] Quoted in "The Reagan Years: Regrouping on Education," *Science*, November 1980, p. 991.

[26] Quoted in "There Will Be No Dominance of Education," *U.S. News & World Report*, May 12, 1980, p. 51.

[27] As is provided for under Title I of the Elementary and Secondary Education Act of 1965. This act, with 15 titles, is the main body of federal education legislation below the college level.

aid one segment of education, possibly at the expense of another. But regardless of philosophic underpinnings, the federal interest in private education has been growing for some time. The Department of Education's National Center for Education Statistics now gathers information on private schools, and there is a position in the department, though unfilled, that deals only with private schools.

Developments in private education itself are reinforcing federal research interest. The recently formed Council for American Private Education, a Washington-based advocacy group, is the first of its kind. The American Education Research Association now includes a private school study group — Associates for Research on Private Education — and the University of San Francisco recently organized a new private school research organization, the Center for Research on Private Education.

Except for a few federally funded programs, private education has received public support mostly through tax exemptions and deductions. At the state and local level, private schools usually are not required to pay property taxes. Neither do most private schools, as non-profit corporations, pay income, use or sales taxes. Individuals and corporations may also deduct contributions to private institutions from their income taxes, and private non-profit schools receive special mailing privileges.

The U.S. tax code's relationship with private education has sometimes been stormy. This was especially true of the Internal Revenue Service's dealings with Southern private schools that came into being to circumvent federal civil rights legislation in the early days of desegregation. In 1970, the U.S. District Court for the District of Columbia ruled in *Green v. Connally* that racially discriminatory schools in Mississippi were not entitled to tax exemptions. The decision was later upheld by the Supreme Court, and in 1975 the IRS provided its first set of guidelines for schools that wished to retain their exempt status.

Christian schools have long been wary of federal control through IRS provisions. Their great fear has been that if tax breaks are counted as federal assistance, then the government may assume the right to demand compliance on other rules that apply to schools receiving direct aid. They fear federal interference with curriculum, licensing, school hours and attendance.[28]

Tax Credit Measures in States and Localities

While attention has been focused on the federal government, tuition tax credit proposals have been introduced in one form or another in several states and in the District of Columbia. The

---

[28] See Edd Doerr, "Tuition Tax Credits: Threat to Religious Liberty and Public Education," Americans United for Separation of Church and State.

D.C. Elections Board recently refused a place on the November 1981 ballot for the city's voters to decide if they wanted the local government to provide tax reimbursement for half of the tuition to private schools — elementary, secondary or college — up to $1,200 a year per student, through city income tax credits. Through petitions — the initiative procedure — local citizens with National Taxpayers Union backing sought unsuccessfully to force a reluctant city administration to bring the question to a vote. Opponents of tuition tax credits charged that the National Taxpayers Union was using the District of Columbia as a laboratory for an initiative that the organization sponsored but withdrew in California last year.

E. G. West, of the Heritage Foundation, reasoned that the shift from California to the District of Columbia might be explained by a current California initiative attempt to establish a voucher system in that state. "To many who wish to see the principle of family choice adopted," West said, "the existence of two competing schemes in one state would appear to have the misfortune of splitting the vote." Now that the California tax credit has been dropped, "the way seems clear for the voucher system to obtain the requisite number of supporters."[29] "Voucher education," as envisioned in California, would give parents a voucher entitling them to receive payment for most of the cost of educating their children at a school of their choosing, public or private.[30]

Still another type of subsidy, a tax deduction for the cost of schooling, has been at issue in Minnesota and Rhode Island. Whereas a tax credit permits the taxpayer to subtract it directly from the amount he owes the government, the degree of benefit he receives from a deduction is in relation to his income. Because of the graduated income tax system, a deduction benefits the rich more than the poor. A $1,000 deduction for someone in the 50 percent tax bracket would mean a saving of $500. But a taxpayer in the 20 percent bracket would receive only a $200 benefit. Both the Minnesota and Rhode Island laws are currently undergoing court challenges.

The Montana legislature this year killed a bill to provide tax credits to corporations and individuals for donations to private schools, and a bill to provide $16 million worth of textbooks to parochial schools was defeated in Texas.

The organization Americans United for Separation of Church and State has counted 10 statewide referenda on government aid for private schools conducted in nine states between 1967 and 1976, and reports all were voted down. The record of

---

[29] E. G. West, *op. cit.*, p. 51.
[30] For background, see "Private School Resurgence," *E.R.R.*, 1979 Vol. I, pp. 299-302.

defeats can be interpreted as majority opposition to tax aid for non-public schools, especially church-related schools. A poll conducted by the Gallup organization last spring for *Newsweek* is further evidence of the attitude. Gallup reported that 52 percent of the people it questioned nationwide opposed tuition tax credits while only 34 percent favored them.[31]

On the other hand, times may be changing. There is the mounting belief, and bits of buttressing evidence cited throughout this report, that as the middle class increasingly finds public schools unsatisfactory it will become more amendable to a tax-supported alternative. Indeed, the number of federal, state and local tax-aid questions is a sign of building pressure. And more pressure, rather than less, can be expected.

---

[31] See "The Bright Flight," *Newsweek*, April 20, 1981, p. 68.

Selected Bibliography

Books

Mosher, Edith, K. and Jennings L. Wagoner, Jr., eds., *The Changing Politics of Education: Prospects for the 1980's*, McCutchan, 1978.

Articles

"The Bright Flight," *Newsweek*, April 20, 1981.
"A Case for Moral Absolutes," *Time*, June 8, 1981.
Church & State, selected issues.
Doyle, Denis P., "Public Policy and Private Education, *Phi Delta Kappan*, September 1980.
The Forensic Quarterly (published by Program and Discussion and Debate, National University Extension Association), spring 1981.
Hollings, Ernest F., "The Case Against Tuition Tax Credits," *The New Republic*, December 1978.
Merrow, John, "The Tuition Tax Dodge," *The New Republic*, April 18, 1981.
Moynihan, Daniel Patrick, "Government and the Ruin of Private Education," *Harper's*, April 1978.
"The Public School Lobby Fends Off Tuition Tax Credits — At Least for Now," *National Journal*, June 13, 1981.

Reports and Studies

Abramowitz, Susan and others, "The Private High School Today," National Institute of Education, 1980.
Coleman, James, "Public and Private Schools," National Center for Education Statistics, 1981.
Editorial Research Reports: "Private School Resurgence," 1979 Vol. I, p. 287.
Greeley, Andrew M., "Minority Students in Catholic Secondary Schools," Ford and Spencer Foundations, 1981.
Nehrt, Roy C., "Private Schools in American Education," National Center for Education Statistics, 1981.
West, E. G., "The Economics of Education Tax Credits," The Heritage Foundation, 1981.

Mainstreaming: Handicapped Children in the Classroom

by

William V. Thomas

July 24
1 9 8 1

MAINSTREAMING: HANDICAPPED CHILDREN IN THE CLASSROOM

HANDICAPPED CHILDREN have been called the country's most oppressed minority. Whether blind, deaf, crippled or retarded, they are the victims of both sympathy and neglect. Although analogies have been made between their situation and that of blacks in the past, it is argued that racial minorities were never as stigmatized or misunderstood as the disabled. Handicapped children "are distributed randomly so that most have able-bodied parents," explained psychologist John Gliedman. "They are parachuted into an able-bodied world. So there is no community of disabled people in which such a child can grow up, no cultual support system, no accumulated body of wisdom." Identified by the handicapped role alone, they "are stripped of their social being [and] reduced to mere biology."[1]

But the problem is not so much a matter of biology as it is one of perception. "Disabled children are handicapped by the public's attitude toward them," said Jeptha V. Greer, director of the Council for Exceptional Children in Reston, Va. By labeling them as "defective," society frees itself of the responsibility for excluding disabled children from normal activities and pursuits — from schools, jobs and a meaningful place in life. The result, Greer said, "is a terrible waste."[2]

No one knows for certain how many Americans are disabled, but estimates range up to 50 million people. Children are thought to make up approximately 20 percent of the total. In years past, most handicapped children received little, if any, education. Those that did rarely attended public schools, which, for the most part, were either unwilling or unable to meet their needs. However, considerable changes have taken place recently in the way public schools deal with handicapped youngsters.[3] Largely because of two federal laws governing the rights of the disabled, handicapped children are now being identified in greater numbers, given more specialized attention, and, in many cases, being put into the same classrooms with "normal" children.

[1] Quoted in *The New York Times,* Feb. 25, 1980.
[2] Interview, July 8, 1981. The Council for Exceptional Children, founded in 1922, works to advance the education of exceptional children and youth, both handicapped and gifted.
[3] See "Rights of the Handicapped," *E.R.R.,* 1974 Vol. II, pp. 885-904.

The first of the laws is Section 504 of the Rehabilitation Act of 1973, which requires easier access to school facilities. The second is the Education for All Handicapped Children Act of 1975, which mandates that public schools provide special programs for all of the nation's disabled children. Together these laws have begun the process of integrating — or "mainstreaming" — handicapped children into the nation's public school population. The aim is to place disabled students in the "least restrictive environment" consistent with their educational requirements. This means that institutionalized children may be transferred to special classes in regular public schools, or that children formerly in special classes in public schools may spend part of their time "mainstreamed" in regular classes.

Mainstreaming is seen by its proponents as the most effective way to educate the handicapped and non-handicapped alike. "It enables children who may have once been seen only in terms of their disability to receive the best education they can," said Peggy Meyer of Mainstream, Inc., a lobbying group for the handicapped. "But mainstreaming also lets non-disabled children see and be with disabled kids, and hopefully learn to accept them for what they are, not for what they appear to be."[4] Yet mainstreaming also has its opponents. Many teachers regard it as an excessive burden in already overcrowded classrooms. Parents often question its educational value. And at a time of reduced federal aid to schools, a growing number of educators who otherwise sympathize with its goals say it is simply too expensive.

Official Count of Handicapped Students

Closely related to the cost of mainstreaming is the question of exactly how many handicapped children there are, for the count affects how much money is appropriated and determines how it will be distributed to the states *(see p. 32)*. According to the federal Office of Special Education (OSE), over 4.1 million handicapped children were served by state and local education agencies during the 1980-1981 school year — 8.65 percent of the school-age population.[5] The largest group of handicapped children were the 1.4 million with learning disabilities. Children with speech impairments (1.1 million) and mental retardation (852,061) constituted the second and third largest groups. Five smaller categories accounted for the remainder of the children served *(see box, p. 31)*.

Despite stepped-up efforts to identify handicapped children, counting them is more of an art than a science. On a continuum of handicapping conditions, it is easy to categorize those on the

---

[4] Interview, July 10, 1981.
[5] The school-age population includes children ages 6 through 17.

Disabled children are handicapped by the public's attitude toward them.

ends of the scale — those who are clearly handicapped, or clearly not. But in between, the distinction between a handicapped and non-handicapped condition can get very fuzzy. The hazy definitions of a handicap, particularly for categories such as learning disability and emotional disturbance, open up a wide range of discretion for the people doing the counting.

Some schools and teachers are said to be reluctant to report handicapped children, as the law requires, because of the work and expense involved. School administrators say that the cost of complying with all the requirements for a reported child are too much compared with the modest federal reimbursement. Still another problem arises from the social and cultural biases involved in assessing the handicapped.

Such biases are sometimes related to the attitudes of parents in different social classes toward the handicapped conditions of their children. This helps to explain at least one apparent anomaly. The highest identification rates tend to be in those communities where most medical evidence suggests they should be the lowest. Some middle-class areas, where relatively good health and nutrition would be expected to help reduce handicapped conditions, often report large numbers of children served.

One reason for this is thought to be the recent upsurge of interest in learning disabilities *(see box, p. 27)*. The diagnosis of a learning disability has a strong attraction for middle-class parents, some educators believe, since it offers an explanation of a child's poor performance in school that does not classify him or her as having a low intelligence. It is much nicer to think of Johnny as being dyslexic than as being "dumb" or poorly motivated. These middle-class parents have the resources and knowledge to ensure that their children are tested for learning disabilities. Low-income parents, by contrast, are frequently more willing to accept their child's poor performance as unavoidable and are more reluctant to seek special help.

Resistance and Implementation Problems

The latest figures available from the Office of Special Education indicated that 68 percent of school-aged handicapped children were being taught in regular public school classes. Approximately one-quarter were in separate classes within regular schools; the rest in separate schools or other educational institutions.[6] The extent of mainstreaming varies widely according to handicapping conditions. Nine out of 10 children with speech impairments, for instance, attend regular classes, usually with a visit sometime during the school day to a speech therapist. On the other hand, less than half of the deaf and hearing impaired are in regular classes; over a quarter are in separate schools or other learning environments.

Implementation of the least restrictive environment requirement has posed severe problems for some states. The OSE notes that resistance to mainstreaming is particularly evident in school districts lacking any previous history of serving disabled students. "In the past, most educators felt that the institutional setting was best suited to serve the needs of disabled children. But we have to overcome this categorical mind set," said Shirley Jones, acting deputy director of the Office of Special Education. "Of course, there are many factors involved in this. The most important is getting the appropriate support services in place to facilitate the movement of students into the most suitable learning environment."[7]

---

[6] The latest available statistics compiled by the federal Office of Special Education for the 1978-79 school year.
[7] Interview, July 14, 1981.

Learning Disabilities

Leonardo da Vinci, Woodrow Wilson, Albert Einstein, Winston Churchill and Igor Sikorsky all had one thing in common. Besides being remarkable achievers, each, as a child, had a learning disability. It is possible, educators say, to find children with learning disabilities who are extremely talented in artistic, mechanical or musical areas. In other words, having a learning problem does not necessarily mean that a child is not intelligent. In fact, it may mean just the opposite.

A recent study by educational psychologist M. B. Rawson indicated that grade school students suffering from dyslexia — a reading problem marked by the tendency to transpose words and letters — were just as likely to succeed in later life as their non-dyslexic classmates.

What makes some learning disabilities difficult to treat is the psychological problems they cause. A common trait among many children with learning disabilities is a negative self-image. The children "feel that parents as well as teachers lower their expectations in all areas when they discover the handicap," learning specialist C. June Maker wrote in *Providing Programs for the Gifted Handicapped* (1977).

It is this lowering of expectations, educators contend, that often presents the most difficult obstacle to overcome. "You have to program success into everything you teach these children," said Cleveland reading teacher Carol Gandal. "It is the main thing they've been deprived of and need so desperately to experience."

Much of the burden for providing these services has fallen on classroom teachers who often do not have the special training needed to cope with the handicapped children in their classes. Consequently, some teachers have felt overwhelmed by their new responsibilities. Others have felt they were being forced to slight their non-handicapped children in order to cope with the disabled students.

In practice, mainstreaming has proven more workable with physically disabled children and with those of normal intelligence who have learning disabilities. But it has posed significant difficulties with retarded students or those with social and emotional problems. In most cases teachers have shown themselves willing to put up with severe physical disabilities as long as the child is a normal learner. The problems come with students who are prone to be disruptive and present classroom management problems.

One obvious solution is better training of teachers, and most school districts are making efforts in this direction. Another response has been for some schools to slow down the search for handicapped students while they develop experience in implementing mainstreaming. In contrast to this deliberate ap-

Sources of Information on Handicapped Education

Architectural and Transportation Barriers Compliance Board U.S. Department of Health and Human Services 330 C St., S.W. Washington, D.C. 20201	Monitors compliance with parts of the Rehabilitation Act related to architectural and transportation barriers.
Center for Independent Living 2539 Telegraph Ave. Berkeley, Calif. 94704	Works for the integration of handicapped people into the community.
Closer Look National Information Center for the Handicapped 1201 16th St., N.W. Washington, D.C. 20036	Furnishes information about the education of the disabled.
Council for Exceptional Children 1920 Association Dr. Reston, Va. 22091	Supports research and training aimed at improving the education of handicapped children.
Mainstream Inc. 200 15th St., N.W. Washington, D.C.	Lobbies for the handicapped. Operates a "Call for Compliance" hot line.
National Arts and the Handicapped Information Service Box 2040 Grand Central Station New York, N.Y. 10017	Provides information to make arts programs and facilities accessible to the handicapped.
Office for Civil Rights U.S. Department of Health and Human Services 330 Independence Ave., S.W. Washington, D.C. 20201	Monitors compliance with various handicapped education laws.

proach, however, concern has arisen lately that some schools are using mainstreaming as an excuse for not providing the services a handicapped child really needs. It may seem easier and cheaper to put the children in the back of the class and forget about them than to arrange special instruction.

Individualized Instruction Requirement

One provision of the Education for All Handicapped Children Act requires preparation of an individualized education program (IEP) for each handicapped child. An IEP is a written statement of a child's current educational performance, annual goals and short-term objectives for his or her instruction, plus a list of specific educational services to be provided. IEPs are developed in meetings between administrators, teachers and parents. "The purpose," said Shirley Jones, "is to promote individualized programing and placement."

The IEPs initially met with resistance from teachers and administrators who said preparation of the plans was time-consuming and required too much paperwork. Also many educators resented the interference of parents in areas within their professional purview. The vast number of handicapped children now have such programs. But in some cases compliance has been mixed and the quality of the programs doubtful. Certain school districts have been found to be sending standardized forms to students' homes for the parents to sign. In other cases, special education teachers complain that what is supposed to be a combined effort on the part of regular classroom teachers, parents and school administrators is routinely passed on to them.

Although most teachers are getting used to IEPs, "there are still tremendous problems," said Dena Stoner of the National School Boards Association. Much of the work involved in preparing individual objectives is so complicated, she said, that "there are long waiting lists in many areas just for children to have their initial evaluation."[8] The problem is likely to get worse before it gets better. As techniques for identifying disabled students become more sophisticated, more children will need to be served by schools and current problems will be compounded. "What we're seeing now is only the tip of the iceberg," Stoner said.

Educational opportunities for handicapped children are increasing. Still, various sources estimate that around 20 percent of all disabled students never go beyond the eighth grade. More schools at all levels are accepting handicapped children, but officials continue to grumble that they are being forced to use scarce resources on behalf of a relatively small number of children.

Decade of Legal Battles

THE FIRST skirmish in the struggle over handicapped education came in January 1971, when the Pennsylvania Association for Retarded Children (PARC), on behalf of 14 retarded school-age youngsters representing all other such children in the state, filed a class-action suit against the Commonwealth of Pennsylvania. The suit charged that the state had failed to provide access to free public education for all retarded children. The legal battle lasted a year. In the court decree, reached by consent agreement, the state department of education pledged

[8] Interview, July 14, 1981.

to stop excluding children from public school programs because of their mental retardation, and not to shift children from regular to special classes without advance parental notice and a formal due process hearing. This included the right to legal counsel and the right to present evidence, such as independent medical, psychological and educational evaluations. Finally, the department agreed to seek out all retarded youths between the ages of 6 and 21 in the state, and offer them access to education and training as soon as possible.

Some educators saw the PARC decision as an isolated ruling. But within a year another decision went even farther. The case was *Mills v. Board of Education,* which was decided in August 1972 in the U.S. District Court in Washington, D.C. It is now considered a milestone in the right to education movement. The parents and guardians of seven children in the District of Columbia brought a class-action suit charging the city with failure to provide the children with a free public education. The children had handicaps including brain damage, hyperactivity, epilepsy, mental retardation and an orthopedic problem. The court ruled that the Constitution required individually appropriate public education for all children, regardless of their handicaps.

These cases were soon followed by others. Between 1971 and 1975, when Congress passed the Education for All Handicapped Children Act, right-to-education suits were filed in more than 25 states. As a result, some state legislatures passed laws requiring a free public education for all handicapped children,[9] while others made state funds available for special education programs. According to the Council for Exceptional Children, increases in state appropriations between the 1971-72 and the 1973-74 school years ranged from 15 percent in Maine to 377 percent in West Virginia. In addition, Congress acted to guarantee the right to education through federal law. The Education Act of 1974 declared that "every citizen is entitled to meet his or her full potential without financial barriers...." This measure also authorized federal grants to states totaling $630 million for special education programs.

Federal Help for Handicapped Children

Prompted by an increasing number of court cases finding that handicapped children had a right to be educated, Congress in 1975 passed the Education for All Handicapped Children Act aimed at assuring them adequate public schooling. Under the law, states were required to provide a free education to all their disabled children. The legislation required that first priority be

---

[9] These states included Arkansas, Florida, Maine, Missouri, New York, North Carolina, West Virginia and Wisconsin.

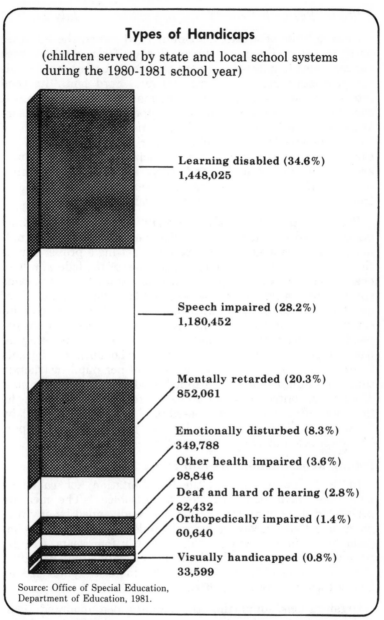

Types of Handicaps

(children served by state and local school systems during the 1980-1981 school year)

Learning disabled (34.6%)
1,448,025

Speech impaired (28.2%)
1,180,452

Mentally retarded (20.3%)
852,061

Emotionally disturbed (8.3%)
349,788

Other health impaired (3.6%)
98,846

Deaf and hard of hearing (2.8%)
82,432

Orthopedically impaired (1.4%)
60,640

Visually handicapped (0.8%)
33,599

Source: Office of Special Education,
Department of Education, 1981.

given to children who were not currently receiving an education and that second priority be given to those with the most severe handicaps. It stipulated that federal funds be used only to pay the excess cost of educating handicapped children — that is, the state and local school district would first have to spend as much money on each handicapped child as they did on other children. The act also strengthened existing due process procedures to guarantee the rights of handicapped children.

Despite hints of a veto, President Ford signed the bill after both houses of Congress approved a conference report with enough votes to guarantee a veto override. "Unfortunately this bill promises more than it can deliver," Ford said. "Its good intentions could be thwarted by the many unwise provisions it contains.... Even the strongest supporters of this measure know as well as I that they are falsely raising the expectations of the groups affected by claiming authorization levels which are excessive and unrealistic."[10] Ford criticized the measure's "vast array of detailed, complex and costly administrative requirements which would unnecessarily assert federal control over traditional state and local government functions."

Passage of the act represented a significant change in national policy toward educating the handicapped. Convinced that millions of handicapped children were not getting a proper education, sponsors of the bill won an expansion of the federal role to ensure that states lived up to their responsibilities. In the same spirit, Congress set an ambitious schedule of increasing levels of assistance to states and local schools to help handicapped education. The idea was that the federal commitment would expand along with the national requirements for educating all handicapped children. The law set the level of authorized grants to states according to the average cost of per-pupil instruction times the number of handicapped students served by states. The federal contribution was to be 5 percent of this amount the first year after the act was passed, and grow to 40 percent by fiscal year 1982. But since the law was passed, federal support has never risen above 12 percent (see p. 35).

Putting Rehabilitation Act into Effect

In 1973, Congress passed the Rehabilitation Act, called by many the "civil rights act for the disabled." The measure prohibited discrimination against the handicapped by any program or activity receiving federal funds. But progress on implementing the law was stalled for nearly four years. Regulations were drawn up by the Ford administration, but President Carter on taking office in 1977 said that more study was needed before they were put into effect.

Organizations supporting the handicapped mounted demonstrations across the country to pressure the Carter administration to implement the law. This tactic apparently worked. In April 1977, Joseph A. Califano Jr., the secretary of health, education and welfare, signed the regulations. He summarized their importance as follows: This "represents the first federal civil rights law protecting the rights of handicapped persons and reflects a national commitment to end discrimination on the

---

[10] Statement released by the White House, Dec. 2, 1975.

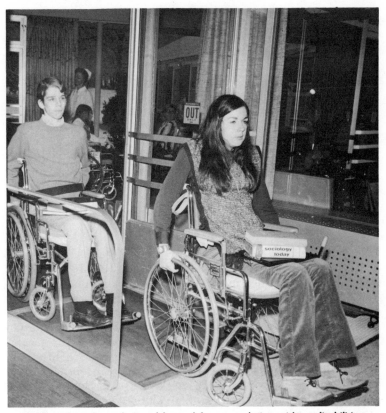

Buildings have been designed by and for a population without disabilities.

basis of handicap. The language ... is almost identical to the comparable non-discrimination provisions of Title VI of the Civil Rights Act of 1964 and Title IX of the Education Amendments of 1972 [applying to racial discrimination and to discrimination in education on the basis of sex]. It establishes a mandate to end discrimination and bring handicapped persons into the mainstream of American life."[11]

Under the regulations, schools receiving federal funds had to make all new buildings accessible to handicapped persons and had to ensure that all programs in existing buildings were accessible. If program accessibility could not be accomplished, existing programs had to be modified within three years. In addition, the regulations required that all handicapped children be provided with a free education, in their neighborhood school if possible. Universities were prohibited from discriminating against handicapped persons in any area of university life.

In the past, disabled children were frequently placed in segregated, special schools. But this type of schooling, it was ar-

[11] Speaking in Washington, April 28, 1977.

gued, had profound negative effects on a child's self-image as well as his ability to learn. As did the civil rights legislation of the 1960s, the civil rights laws for the disabled rejected the concept of a segregated education. "The premise and the promise of these laws is that the disabled child can and will succeed in the public school system," wrote Edward V. Roberts, director of rehabilitation for the state of California. "They offer a hope to the parent of the disabled child who has found the school door closed. Integrated schools can remove what is one of the greatest obstacles facing the children with disabilities — the absence of opportunities for socialization. It will enable them to work and play with their non-disabled peers and to gain social skills and behavior patterns that are critical to their personal fulfillment as adults."[12]

Effort to Remove Architectural Barriers

One of the most controversial parts of the Rehabilitation Act was Section 504, which mandated that federally funded institutions, including schools, make all their facilities physically accessible to the handicapped. This rule recognized that buildings historically have been designed by and for a population without disabilities. Under the 504 regulations, specific accommodations would be determined by the facts of each situation. In schools, that meant that elevators had to be provided for students in wheelchairs, braille markers had to be put in place for blind students, and adjustable volume telephones supplied for students whose hearing was impaired.

Although some schools and colleges had already embarked on voluntary efforts to remove architectural barriers, many educators feared the cost of making the required alterations would be enormous. The problem was — and remains — particularly serious for older schools in crowded urban areas, where buildings tend to be multi-storied and designed without much thought to the handicapped. Newer schools in less congested areas tend to be spread out on one level, and thus are much more accessible to the movement-impaired.

Under the terms of the law, schools did not have to make every room accessible. What they did have to do was make sure that all educational and extra-curricular programs were available to the disabled. In other words, schools were not required to have an elevator in every building. But they did have to make sure that the only German course, for example, did not meet in an inaccessible classroom.

By and large, educators supported the intent of the rules on accommodation. However, most complained about the funding

---

[12] Edward V. Roberts, "Into The Mainstream: The Civil Rights of People with Disabilities," *Civil Rights Digest*, winter 1979, p. 24.

procedures — or to be more specific, the failure of the federal government to reimburse them fully for what Congress ordered them to spend. The requirements of Section 504 differed from those of the Education for All Handicapped Children Act in that they were not accompanied by the promise of federal funds.

The removal of physical barriers was to have been completed by June 2, 1980. But few educators regarded that deadline as enforceable. However, according to Jeptha V. Greer of the Council for Exceptional Children, "just the idea that things had to change got a lot of schools moving in the right direction." The removal of barriers, he said, "was resisted by some people at first. But it's been shown that affording the disabled access to schooling — aside from the human rights aspect — is really a way to save money. It helps to make the handicapped contributing members of society rather than an economic burden."

Future Funding and Direction

U NDER the Education for All Handicapped Children Act, federal funds were expected to cover 40 percent of the excess cost of educating disabled students by 1982. But Congress has never appropriated enough money to meet its commitment. The portion of the cost covered by federal funds currently stands at slightly under 12 percent. And indications are that by next year it will be even lower. A central problem in the future of handicapped education is how the states and local school districts will comply with federal law without receiving all the federal funding they were promised.

The final 1981 appropriation, signed into law in June, cut $80 million in federal aid for handicapped education grants to the states.[13] Advocates of increased funding argue that this cut will stretch school budgets to the breaking point. "There's a feeling of betrayal among educators," said Thomas A. Shannon, executive director of the National School Boards Association. "There's also a feeling that the federal government has acted hypocritically. It set up the programs, then told the schools to pay for them. Then it cuts funding, but doesn't reduce the mandates. We're definitely in favor of doing all we can for handicapped children. But where's the money supposed to come from?"[14]

---

[13] The legislation signed by President Reagan on June 6 reduced to $874 million the level of handicapped aid in the fiscal 1981 continuing resolution, which expired June 5. The bill, PL 97-12, extends funding for many federal programs, including education, through Sept. 30, the end of the 1981 fiscal year.

[14] Interview, July 14, 1981.

The average cost of educating a handicapped child usually is estimated to be twice the normal cost of instruction. The extra spending required to meet handicapped needs comes in at least four areas:

> For a student whose needs cannot be met within the regular school system, the local school district must provide placement in a special school that can meet those needs, at no expense to the parents. The cost of this special instruction can run into tens of thousands of dollars a year per child.
>
> Special teachers have to be hired to work with handicapped children who remain within the local school system. They generally command higher salaries and work with fewer students than the average teacher.
>
> Regular classroom teachers must be trained to work with the handicapped students in their classes.
>
> And special tests must be given — a time-consuming process — to determine which students are handicapped.

Some school officials are predicting that, in a time of tight budgets, the heavy spending requirements of handicapped education could produce a backlash from regular educators. The lack of adequate federal funding, they say, has already produced more crowded special education classes and longer waiting periods for children to be served. "The courts will always be requiring us to do something," said Shannon. But "the prospect many of our people are facing right now is having to take money out of their general funds to pay for handicapped programs. Obviously, this could lead to all sorts of problems."

Reagan administration officials argue that many schools in the past wasted federal aid. Another administration concern is that certain schools may be using federal funds to pay all their handicapped costs, rather than to pay the excess costs over and above the normal expense of instruction (see p. 31). Whatever the administration does, advocates for handicapped rights argue that states and schools still have to meet their obligations under the law, even if they do not get all the help they would like.

Criticism of Administration's Approach

Last month, Congress modified an administration proposal that would have consolidated funds for handicapped children with a number of other educational aid programs. The compromise measure kept handicapped programs more or less intact. But many educators, who believe that Reagan wants to greatly diminish federal participation in education, think the handwriting is on the wall. "We're taking Ronald Reagan at his word," said Thomas Shannon. "He envisions a reduced role for government, and that probably will mean more cuts in spending and more pressure on schools to make do."

1981 Budget for Special Education and Rehabilitative Services

	Final 1981 Appropriations
Education for the Handicapped and Gifted and Talented	
Education for the Handicapped (State Assistance)	
State grant program	$ 874,500,000
Preschool incentive grants	25,000,000
Deaf-blind centers	16,000,000
Special population programs	
Severely handicapped projects	4,375,000
Early childhood education	17,500,000
Vocational programs	2,950,000
Innovation and development	15,000,000
Media services	17,000,000
Resource centers	7,656,000
Recruitment	750,000
Personnel development	43,500,000
Special studies	1,000,000
Gifted and talented	5,652,000
Subtotal	1,030,883,000
Rehabilitative Services and Handicapped Research	
Rehabilitative Services	
Basic state grants	854,259,000
Innovation and expansion	———
Service projects	29,860,000
Independent living	18,000,000
Training	21,675,000
Subtotal	923,794,000
National Institute of Handicapped Research	29,750,000
National Council on the Handicapped	205,000
Total	1,984,632,000
Total Department of Education Budget	$14,273,433,000

Source: Department of Education, 1981.

Central to the administration's strategy is the substitution of educational block grants for categorical grants.[15] Critics warn that block grants could doom some of the major federal education programs of the past two decades. When he proposed the block grants in March, Reagan said they would give state and local officials more control over how federal education funds are spent in their communities, and would end burdensome federal

---

[15] Block grants are made for broadly designed purposes. While the money must be spent on programs in a general area, state or local officials may make decisions on how the money is actually distributed. Categorical grants, on the other hand, can be used only for specific programs as directed by Congress and the federal agencies.

Center for Independent Living

During the 1960s, Berkeley, Calif., became a mecca for radical activities. The free-speech movement started there, as did the anti-war and anti-draft movements. At the same time, however, Berkeley was becoming the center for another, less visible struggle — an effort to liberate the nation's millions of handicapped persons from the impediments that circumscribe their daily lives.

The movement began in 1962 when Edward V. Roberts, a quadriplegic, enrolled as the University of California's first full-time disabled student. Disabled students now enrolled at the school number more than 400, with 150 of them in wheelchairs. This gives Berkeley the largest concentration of handicapped people on any campus in the country.

To help in their adaptation, the handicapped students and others joined together to set up the Center for Independent Living (CIL) in 1972. The center is the hub of handicapped activity in Berkeley and has served as a model for other such facilities elsewhere. In addition to counseling services, the center helps area handicapped persons acquire skills that permit them to live independently. The CIL operates a 24-hour-a-day wheel-chair repair service, modifies cars and vans so they might be driven by the handicapped, and runs a special attendant referral program. The center also works to overturn laws that it believes discriminate against the disabled.

regulations and paperwork that educators have long complained about. Funding cuts, he said, would be offset by administrative savings.

Groups representing handicapped children strongly oppose cutbacks in the programs and their funding. They fear that without restrictions on how federal money is used, supporters of the various programs will fight among themselves for a shrinking pot of funds. Programs with the least political clout may not survive, they warn. Critics of the administration's block grant approach also fear that states will simply use the money to replace their own spending on education instead of supplementing it, as existing law requires.

The Reagan administration has countered these arguments with a plea for faith in the good will of local officials. Local people know what is best for their students and will continue to fund necessary programs — if for no other reason than they would not want to take the political heat for failing to serve poor or handicapped children, Education Secretary T. H. Bell has argued. But so far, supporters of education for the handicapped have not been persuaded. They note that the reason most federal education programs were created was that states and localities were unwilling or unable to provide them. They also say that federal safeguards are necessary to be sure that children continue to get the special help they need.

If the Reagan proposals are ever adopted, education programs for disabled children would fall far short of any meaningful experience, said Thomas Gilhool, a lawyer specializing in handicapped rights cases. "The question is not whether disabled kids would be in school or not, but whether in school they will [get any instruction] worth having."[16]

"The full range of services disabled students require cannot be delivered by [local] school boards alone."

Samuel Bonham, president
of the National Association
of State Directors of Special
Education

With the administration cutting back assistance and the courts increasing their responsibilities toward handicapped students, many education officials think too much is being asked of them. Citing recent court decisions ordering schools to provide year-round special services for disabled students, Bernetta Bush, a lawyer for the Illinois Department of Education, said that judges apparently "seem to think that anything that relates to a child is necessary for their education." Bush predicted that without more federal aid and a greater distribution of the burden among local agencies, the heyday of optimal services for handicapped children will soon end.

Although few educators want to see the handicapped rights laws obliterated, most agree that it is time to review the myriad rules and regulations drawn up to interpret them. "Let's keep the principles of the law," said Samuel Bonham, president of the National Association of State Directors of Special Education. But, he added, the courts, Congress and the president should realize that the full range of services disabled students require "cannot be delivered by school boards alone."[17]

---

[16] Speaking in Washington, D.C., at the National Institute on Legal Problems of Educating the Handicapped, May 10, 1981.
[17] Bonham and Bush also were addressing the National Institute on Legal Problems of Educating the Handicapped.

Selected Bibliography

Books

Bowe, Frank, *Handicapping America: Barriers to Disabled People,* Harper & Row, 1978.

Brewer, Garry D. and James S. Kakalik, *Handicapped Children: Strategies for Improving Service,* McGraw-Hill, 1978.

Bruck, Lilly, *Access, The Guide to a Better Life for Disabled Americans,* Random House, 1979.

Hale, Glorya, ed., *The Source Book for the Disabled,* Paddington Press, 1979.

Heisler, Verda, *Handicapped Child in the Regular Classroom,* Grune Press, 1976.

Kershaw, John D., *Handicapped Children,* International Ideas, 1976.

Reamy, Louis, *Travelability,* Macmillan, 1978.

Articles

"Cost Problems Plague Transit for the Disabled," *Business Week,* July 3, 1978.

The Independent (a publication of the Center for Independent Living, a California program for disabled persons), selected issues.

"New Products: A Boon to the Disabled," *U.S. News & World Report,* Aug. 28, 1978.

Roberts, Edward V., "Into the Mainstream: The Civil Rights of People with Disabilities," *Civil Rights Digest,* winter 1979.

The Chronicle of Higher Education, selected issues.

Walker, Lisa, "Fund Limits and Special Education: Mandates are Mandates," *Compact,* spring 1979.

Reports and Studies

Editorial Research Reports: "Rights of the Handicapped," 1974 Vol. II, p. 885.

National Association of State Directors of Special Education, "An Analysis of P.L. 94-142," 1975.

The Council for Exceptional Children, "Public Law 94-142 and Section 504 — Understanding What They Are and Are Not," 1977.

U.S. Department of Health, Education and Welfare, "Progress Toward a Free Appropriate Public Education," January 1979.

Cover art by Staff Artist Robert Redding; photo on p. 25 by Nanda Ward Haynes for the Council for Exceptional Children; photo on p. 33 courtesy of the U.S. Department of Health and Human Services.

PLIGHT OF AMERICA'S BLACK COLLEGES

by

William V. Thomas

RR '81

**Jan. 23
1 9 8 1**

Editor's Note: Since this Report was published early in 1981, Congress at the urging of the Reagan administration has reduced several college aid programs. Perhaps the most important for black private schools is the so-called Pell grant program, providing annual awards — in contrast to loans — to needy students. The size of these grants was reduced from $1,750 a year to $1,670, 1981-82 academic year. Many students at black colleges are unable to obtain federally subisidized low-interest loans. Typically the students are from rural areas where the local banks do not participate in the loan program.

PLIGHT OF AMERICA'S BLACK COLLEGES

TO SOME of those present, the scene must have brought back memories of days gone by, of civil rights marches and fiery rhetoric, of blacks bringing their message to the nation's capital. But times have changed. The thousands of protesters who demonstrated at Black College Day in Washington last September were there not to denounce segregation but rather in a sense to demand it. The issue was preserving historically black schools, whose existence many believe is threatened by a "blind" commitment to integration and a growing neglect of the educational needs of blacks. Television journalist Tony Brown, who organized the rally, called the challenge to black higher education a clear and present danger. "Without black colleges and universities," he said, "the country would lose more than half of its black college graduates."[1] Other speakers echoed Brown's concern. "We're here to save our kids' minds from extinction," said longtime civil rights activist Dick Gregory.

Since 1970, the black student population at colleges across the nation has increased by 275 percent. According to the latest Census Bureau figures, blacks account for 10 percent of all college students, just slightly below their 13 percent overall proportion in the population.[2] But the traditionally black colleges, which 20 years ago enrolled 96 percent of all black college students, now enroll fewer than 20 percent.

As more black students enter predominantly white institutions, hard-pressed black colleges face a struggle for survival.[3] The integration of black schools by whites and the merger of black state colleges into statewide university systems are seen as threats to their unique identities. Black college officials also complain that the federal government has begun to designate less money for their schools at a time when many of them badly need such assistance to stay in operation (see p. 46).

There are 160 predominantly black colleges in the United

---

[1] Speaking in Washington, September 29, 1980.
[2] Census Bureau statistics for March 1979.
[3] At three historically black institutions, blacks are now in the minority: Lincoln University in Jefferson City, Mo. (37 percent); West Virginia State College (20 percent); and Bluefield State College in West Virginia (16 percent).

States.[4] They range in size from Howard University, in Washington, D.C., with nearly 10,000 students, to Natchez Junior College, in Mississippi, which had only 35 students in 1980. Of the 212,000 students enrolled in black colleges in 1976, 88 percent were black and 9 percent, or 18,000, were white.[5]

Black institutions awarded only 4 percent of the 1,213 doctorates gained by blacks in 1976 and only 4 percent of the 41,000 associate or two-year degrees. But they awarded 20 percent of the 2,700 professional degrees in law and medicine, 22 percent of the 20,000 master's degrees and 38 percent of the 59,000 bachelor's degrees blacks received that year.

Addressing the National Association for Equal Opportunity in Higher Education last April, Shirley M. Hufstedler, secretary of education in the Carter administration, assured black college officials that "there is an important place for your schools in American education, one worthy of their proud history." But she also said that black colleges must adjust to the times, including a projected 15 percent decline over the next decade in the number of 18- to 21-year-olds, a "greater competition to enroll black students" by predominantly white schools, and an on-going federal effort to eliminate racial segregation in state college systems.[6]

Having to grapple with some of the issues they themselves raised in the 1960s, supporters of black higher education would seem to have two irreconcilable goals: They want black students to have a fair chance of admission to predominantly white colleges, yet they also want to preserve the racial identity of colleges that long have been predominantly black. But, they point out, these two goals are compatible with a third, overriding one: to give blacks the widest possible opportunity for a college education in an environment suited to their needs.

Support for Maintaining Black Colleges

Sociologists Christopher Jencks and David Riesman, in a 1967 article in *Harvard Educational Review,* called the black college of the mid-20th century "an ill-financed, ill-staffed caricature of white higher education."[7] Other critics more recently have attempted to dismiss arguments for the continuation of black colleges as sentimental examples of ethnic chauvinism. They maintain that there is a qualitative difference between black

---

[4] According to the National Advisory Committee on Black Higher Education, there are 100 "historically" black colleges — those that were founded between 1854 and 1954 for the express purpose of educating blacks. Of these, 39 are public and 61 are private. There are 60 newer predominantly black schools; 31 of them are public and 29 private.
[5] Latest figures available from the National Center for Educational Statistics.
[6] Speaking in Washington, April 12, 1980.
[7] Christopher Jencks and David Riesman, "The American Negro College," *Harvard Educational Review,* winter 1967, p. 27.

Distribution of Black College Students

Type of Institution	Historically Black Colleges	Newer Predominantly Black Colleges	Other Institutions
All Institutions	16.5%	12.9%	70.7%
Public	13.7	14.4	71.9
Private	27.4	6.8	65.8
All Universities	9.0	—	91.0
Public	5.0	—	95.0
Private	18.2	—	81.8
All Four-Year	32.8	5.7	61.5
Public	32.2	7.4	60.4
Private	34.0	2.1	63.9
All Two-Year	1.7	24.6	73.6
Public	1.3	23.5	75.2
Private	8.2	41.8	50.0

Source: National Advisory Committee on Black Higher Education, 1980. Data pertains to 1978.

and white colleges and that black students in black schools receive an inferior education.

There are, of course, many who disagree. Some educators believe black institutions provide a more favorable atmosphere than other schools for educating the so-called "high-risk" student who bears psychological as well as academic handicaps. Such students may be passive inarticulate youths from the rural or small-town South or they may be highly assertive and resentful products of the inner city. The extent to which a sympathetic teaching staff will go to help these students, despite their inadequate preparation for higher learning, is frequently cited as the main educational advantage of the black college.

Traditionally, black college curricula have concentrated on academic "basics." Although the same practice is now being employed at many other schools, "policymakers and educators have seized on this asset of black colleges and have tried by way of reduction to turn it into a liability," said education specialist Charles V. Willie. Some people "have suggested that the future of higher education would be best served if most black colleges became two-year institutions," he added. "But this fails to recognize the other goals that these colleges fulfill. . . . To state it bluntly, black colleges and universities . . . have helped the nation recognize the difference between information and knowledge on the one hand and virtue and wisdom on the other. . . . Black colleges and universities have emphasized these values through sit-ins and freedom rides and civil rights demonstrations led by their students and graduates and through instruction and other means."[8]

Gloomy Financial Picture Getting Worse

Despite recognition of their history and special services, the future of black colleges is in doubt except for some of the strongest among them. The problem is primarily financial. Always supported at a lower level than comparable institutions for whites, black colleges now need increased funds to expand their facilities and services to meet the enlarged scope of black aspirations and to comply with federal guidelines requiring them to attract more white students *(see p. 55)*.

"The financial health and stability of historically black colleges and universities is marginal at best," the National Advisory Committee on Black Higher Education reported last June.[9] Proportionately, black institutions derive less income from student tuition and fees than do other colleges nationwide. As a result, they rely more heavily on public sources of support. But they continue to suffer from fluctuating patterns of federal aid to higher education, the effect of which cannot be offset by their usually meager endowments.

In fiscal year 1975, black colleges derived an average of 17 percent of their revenues from student fees. That compared with a combined average of 25 percent for predominantly white colleges and universities. Black institutions that year received an average of 28 percent of their support from the federal government, compared to 14 percent for white institutions. State contributions to public black and white colleges accounted for 45 and 44 percent of their respective revenues. State support to private black and white colleges came to 1 and 2 percent respectively.

Before passage of the Higher Education Act of 1965, most black colleges and universities were not included in federal programs to assist post-secondary institutions. And there has been little done since then, black educators argue, to rectify past funding inequities. During the period from fiscal year 1970 to fiscal 1974, the black college share of total federal payments to all colleges and universities rose from 3.3 percent to 5.5 percent. It fell to 4.8 percent in fiscal 1975, rose slightly to 4.9 percent in fiscal 1976, and then reached 5.3 percent in fiscal 1977. However, in fiscal year 1978, when federal assistance to all institutions rose 36.5 percent over the previous year, the black college share dropped to 4.1 percent.

---

[8] Charles V. Willie, "Black Colleges Redefined," *Change*, October 1979, p. 47.
[9] National Advisory Committee on Black Higher Education, "Still a Lifeline: The Status of Historically Black Colleges and Universities," June 1980, p. 32.

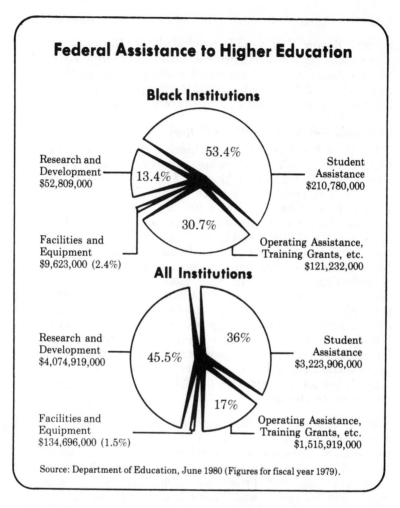

Federal Assistance to Higher Education

Black Institutions

Research and
Development
$52,809,000

13.4%

53.4%

30.7%

Student
Assistance
$210,780,000

Facilities and
Equipment
$9,623,000 (2.4%)

Operating Assistance,
Training Grants, etc.
$121,232,000

All Institutions

Research and
Development
$4,074,919,000

45.5%

36%

17%

Student
Assistance
$3,223,906,000

Facilities and
Equipment
$134,696,000 (1.5%)

Operating Assistance,
Training Grants, etc.
$1,515,919,000

Source: Department of Education, June 1980 (Figures for fiscal year 1979).

According to an unpublished report prepared in 1980 by the Black Initiative Office of the Department of Education, black colleges received only 4.1 percent of the $8.9 billion paid out by 23 selected federal agencies to all colleges and universities in fiscal year 1979. Moreover, only 13.4 percent of federal payments to black colleges that year were earmarked for research and development, while 53.4 percent went for student assistance *(see box, above)*. A total of 45.5 percent of federal funds paid to all institutions in 1979 were for research and development and only 36 percent for student assistance. Black institutions received only 1 percent of all federal funding for research activities.

This discrepancy, along with the overall decrease in black colleges' share of federal payments since 1977 *(see box, p. 57)*, "becomes more dramatic when it is noted that the total dollar amount of federal funds to all institutions rose at least 38 percent during that time," concluded the National Advisory Committee on Black Higher Education. "Clearly, historically black colleges need to command a larger share of federal allocations . . . if they are to continue their pivotal role in preparing black Americans for careers in society."[10]

Increased Racial Tensions on Campuses

If only a handful of the best black colleges survive the economic crunch, what will happen to black students who are forced, as one teacher at Howard University put it, "to sink or swim" at white schools? Dr. Donald Smith of the City University of New York, who has written extensively on the problems blacks encounter at predominantly white schools, predicts most will have a difficult time adjusting to those institutions. Investigating the academic and social problems of black students at the nation's top colleges, Smith discovered a conflicting view between what most blacks believe is important for their cultural and emotional development and what the majority of white faculty and administrators believe is good for the entire institution. The whites Smith interviewed often admitted that their schools represent alienated environments for blacks. Some administrators even confessed to growing tired of socializing young blacks and now want to recruit only "prep-school" blacks who are already able to cope with a predominantly white culture.[11]

Some hold the growing institutional indifference to blacks responsible for the rash of racial incidents at campuses across the country, including such Ivy League schools as Cornell and Harvard, where anti-black sentiments have taken the form of physical attacks and threatening phone calls. At Williams College in Massachusetts and Wesleyan University in Connecticut, racist slogans have been painted on campus buildings. At Purdue University in Indiana there have been at least two Ku Klux Klan-style cross burnings. News of each occurrence has seemed to spawn more demonstrations of hatred, say school authorities, many of whom link the incidents to a resurgence of racism throughout the country. "Because of the current shift in the national mood, I'm assuming that some rather ugly impulses have been liberated," said Wesleyan President Colin Campbell.[12]

While these may be isolated events, psychologists contend their effect on black students, nonetheless, is profound. Al-

---

[10] *Ibid.*, p. 35.
[11] See Donald Smith, "Admissions and Retention Problems of Black Students at Seven Predominantly White Universities," unpublished monograph prepared for the National Advisory Committee on Black Higher Education, 1979. See also "Blacks on Campus," *E.R.R.*, 1972 Vol. II, pp. 665-684.
[12] Quoted in *Time*, Dec. 8, 1980, p. 28.

though there are now over one million blacks studying at predominantly white colleges, one reason for wanting to retain the traditionally black schools is that attending a predominantly white institution can be a traumatic experience for a black student. The theoretical advantages of a more propitious learning environment are too often negated, some educators say, by a frustrating sense of social and cultural isolation. This can produce anger and alienation in blacks whose self-defensive cliquishness in turn can cause resentment in whites. These in themselves are not good reasons for ending efforts at integration, black college spokesmen say, but they do suggest that educational alternatives should be made available to black students who wish to pursue their studies in the more emotionally secure environment a black school offers.

Evolution of Black Colleges

UNTIL after the Civil War, black Americans had only limited access to higher education. Although many colleges in the North were not racially exclusive in the early 1800s, the atmosphere was often inhospitable to blacks and circumstances put many obstacles in the way of their admission. Those blacks who did enroll in predominantly white schools made little overt protest against the character of the institutions they attended or their educational programs and did virtually nothing to influence their reform.

Before black colleges opened, few black Americans received any higher education at all. Only 28 were known to have been awarded bachelor's degrees before the Civil War. In 1826, Amherst College in Massachusetts and Bowdoin College in Maine became the first schools to graduate black students. Harvard did not graduate its first black until 1870, although in earlier years blacks had attended medical classes there. A few theological schools and teacher-training institutions in the North also accepted blacks before the Civil War.

The first all-black college was established outside the South: Cheyney State College in Cheyney, Pa., in 1837. But the South, the home of 90 percent of the nation's black population at the end of the Civil War, was the natural site for the founding of the one-race colleges. The 25 years after the abolition of slavery saw the creation of dozens of black colleges in the Southern and Border states. Most were started through the combined efforts of the Freedmen's Bureau, various church denominations and private philanthropies.

Historians attribute the fervor to establish black colleges to a concern over the morals of ex-slaves and the belief that they were particularly susceptible to frailties of character decried by the Puritan ethic. The churches that sponsored the founding of black colleges — some of which were at the same time establishing other colleges for whites in the South — felt a responsibility to provide some agency of spiritual uplift for blacks. The first heads of these colleges were often men imbued with a strong sense of missionary zeal. Their emphasis was on moral instruction, learning a skill or trade or, in a few cases, preparing for a profession to serve the black community. These goals were spurred by the adoption of the so-called Second Morrill Act of 1890 which provided for the establishment of land-grant colleges for blacks in 17 states.[13]

At first, the post-bellum black colleges were hardly more than grammar schools. Being called a college was more indicative of an ultimate goal than an actuality. Nevertheless, "the fundamental aim of their founders was to build up an enlightened leadership within the race," Howard University sociologist Kelly Miller wrote in 1925. "It was said that the Negro could not be educated. These missionaries refuted that charge by educating him. . . . Experience soon showed that Negro youth fresh from the yoke of slavery could master the white man's knowledge, so-called, in the same length of time and with a comparable degree of thoroughness, as the most favored youth of the most favored race."[14]

Emphasis on Training 'The Talented Tenth'

When Fisk University, now one of the nation's most prestigious black colleges, was founded in Nashville, Tenn., in 1867, most of its classes were in primary grades. As students moved up the grade scale, higher-level instruction was offered. Other black colleges — Howard University in Washington, for example — followed the same pattern. So did a number of colleges for whites founded in the South after the Civil War. Almost to the end of the 19th century, private black colleges retained departments for students unprepared for college-level work.

After segregation in the South was sanctioned by the U.S. Supreme Court in 1896,[15] black colleges became the main source of teachers for the segregated public schools. Thus was "set in motion a complicated supply-demand chain in which the

---

[13] The original Morrill Act of 1862 provided grants of public lands for the establishment of colleges. The name derives from its legislative sponsor, Sen. Justin Smith Morrill, R-Vt.

[14] Kelly Miller, "Howard: The National Negro University," in *The New Negro* (revised edition, 1969), p. 314.

[15] In *Plessy v. Ferguson*, 163 U.S. 537 (1896), the court enunciated the separate-but-equal doctrine. It held that states could compel racial segregation in the use of public facilities, provided that equal facilities were available to all races.

availability of teaching positions — supported however shabbily by the public treasury — drew students into colleges to qualify for the positions. These students in their turn as teachers, expanded the system and sent . . . more students on to the colleges to qualify as teachers."[16]

At the turn of the century, black sociologist and historian W. E. B. DuBois wrote an important essay entitled "The Talented Tenth," in which he argued that the future of the black race in America depended upon the ability of its educated members to lead the masses of their people to positions of productivity and respect in society. DuBois believed that higher education for blacks would produce a Talented Tenth — men and women of intelligence, sympathy and knowledge, who would set the ideals for their community, direct its thoughts and provide moral inspiration and character.

DuBois' theory of racial betterment through a liberal education ran directly counter to the plan advanced by black educator Booker T. Washington. In his cele-brated address at the 1895 Cotton States Exposition in Atlanta, Washington placated white supremacists by renouncing social equality. He urged blacks to make friends with whites but to pursue careers in "agriculture, mechanics . . . and domestic service." In *The Souls of Black Folk* (1903), DuBois called Washington's prescription "a compromise . . . which surrendered the civil and political rights" of blacks. "Mr. Washington," DuBois wrote, "represents in Negro thought the old attitude of adjustment and submission;

Booker T. Washington

but adjustment at such a peculiar time as to make his program unique. This is an age of unusual economic development, and Mr. Washington's [plan] naturally takes an economic cast, but he preaches the gospel of Work and Money to such an extent as to almost overshadow the higher aims in life. . . ."[17]

The Talented Tenth, DuBois believed, embodied those "higher aims." Nevertheless, it was Washington's philosophy of thrift, industry and good manners that enjoyed a wider acceptance among blacks. Washington's influence was a driving force in black education. And nowhere was that influence greater than at Tuskegee (Ala.) Institute, the industrial college he

---

[16] Frank Bowles and Frank A. DeCosta, *Between Two Worlds: A Profile of Negro Higher Education* (1971), p. 36.
[17] W. E. B. DuBois, *The Souls of Black Folk* in *Three Negro Classics* (1965), p. 246.

founded 100 years ago, Feb. 10, 1881. It is unlikely that any
black educators today would subscribe to Washington's policies
of acquiescence in second-class citizenship or his emphasis on
manual training in preference to higher learning and equal
opportunity. But in the early 20th century, Tuskegee Institute
was generally regarded as the best example of what black education should be. Students there were not, at the expense of
industrial instruction, to be educated in the arts, politics or
the professions. For years after Washington's death in 1915
no defections from this strict rule of study and deportment
were ever tolerated.

Black College Unrest During the Twenties

In contrast to the atmosphere of submission that prevailed
at Tuskegee, the decade of the 1920s was a period of unrest
on many black campuses. Students protested disciplinary codes
that made them virtual wards of school presidents. Teachers,
often at the risk of their careers, challenged the prevailing
educational doctrine that stressed vocational training above
liberal arts and relegated faculty members to a position of
vassalage under white administrators. Resistance to change was
firmly entrenched, particularly among church and philanthropic
organizations that had held a tight rein on black higher education since Reconstruction. But by the time strife subsided,
several colleges had been persuaded to elect their first black
presidents; others instituted up-to-date rules of student conduct; and nearly all had taken decisive steps to eliminate the
last vestiges of Booker T. Washington's legacy.

Discontent at Fisk and Howard grew directly out of opposition
to autocratic white presidents. At Fisk students of opposite
sexes were forbidden to meet each other without the presence
and permission of the dean of women or a teacher; co-eds
were required to wear high-neck dresses, cotton stockings and
black hats; and dancing was not allowed. Under the leadership
of W. E. B. DuBois, a Fisk graduate, students began a campaign
in 1923 to abolish these regulations. For two years Fisk's president refused to give ground. Finally, in 1925, a 12-week campus-
wide strike ended in his resignation.

Despite their unprecedented attack on Victorianism, the Fisk
students of the Twenties were hardly radical by the standards
of the 1960s. "They did not dwell on the larger ramifications
of their discontent," wrote historian Raymond Wolters. "Their
focus was on disciplinary rules that were far more stringent
than those at most white colleges . . . and on the basic assumption that Negroes were not prepared to exercise free will."[18]

---

[18] Raymond Wolters, *The New Negro on Campus: Black College Rebellions of the
1920s* (1975), p. 63.

At Howard University grievances centered on the demands of black teachers for a larger role in the management of the school. Of all the black colleges, Howard was generally acknowledged to be the finest. It was, even as early as 1915, a "multiversity" with professional programs and a large annual budget paid for by Congress. Because of its prestige and location in the nation's capital, Howard could attract America's best black scholars. Philosopher Alain Locke, historian Carter Woodson, and sociologist E. Franklin Frazier have been members of Howard's faculty.

"Black colleges represent the best means we have to increase the flow of educated blacks out of disadvantaged positions and into productive roles in society."

Dr. Samuel L. Meyers
January 1981

Howard's professors were "middle-class men who admired family stability and the work ethic and opposed many Negro characteristics as unworthy products of an oppressive environment," Wolters wrote.[19] But, according to E. Franklin Frazier, they also rejected "the servile way in which Negroes imitated the white man's ideals and values and his fear of being different."[20] They insisted that certain aspects of the black subculture should be legitimized, studied and preserved.

Since its founding in 1867, Howard had always been administered by whites. The primary objective of the teachers there was to remove conservative President James Durkee (who simultaneously held the presidency of a segregated Boston school) and replace him with a black man. After a series of firings and behind-the-scenes politicking, the anti-Durkee forces were successful. Whereas students at Fisk had petitioned for wider privileges, Howard's faculty insisted on gaining control of their school. With the election in 1929 of Mordecai Johnson as the univeristy's first black president, they achieved a significant part of their goal.

The later vogue of racial separatism would have been anathema to black college students and teachers of the post-World War I period. Many black students today, Wolters wrote,

---

[19] *Ibid.*, p. 84.
[20] E. Franklin Frazier, "A Note on Negro Education," *Opportunity*, March 1924, p. 75.

"find it hard to compete academically with well prepared whites and fear they cannot survive . . . unless they create sanctuaries that are not subject to traditional academic standards." But black students of the 1920s "demanded an elevated curriculum that would prepare them for full participation in American life."[21]

Integration and Its Academic Side Effects

Throughout the 1930s and 1940s, black colleges remained academic havens where students could receive instruction in the liberal arts and professions that was denied them elsewhere. But with the cracking of racial barriers in education in 1954, when the Supreme Court in its famous *Brown* decision declared separate-but-equal schooling to be unconstitutional, the character of many black institutions began to change. A generation ago, the most promising black students attended black colleges. However, as patterns of discrimination were broken, enrollment trends on black campuses shifted. Black students in increasing numbers entered predominantly white schools, and as a result black colleges suffered.

Since 1979, at least three black colleges have closed.[22] Many of those that survive have become what some have called "academic hospitals." Today, with top students and teachers attracted to predominantly white schools, black institutions are often a last refuge for the economically and educationally disadvantaged — their mission no longer to nurture the "Talented Tenth," but to repair the damage done by poverty and intellectual neglect.

Recently, however, black educators and some of their white colleagues have become involved in a debate over the costs this repair work entails. With federal and state funds for higher education likely to be cut back in coming years, black colleges easily could become an expendable artifact "at the periphery of the educational enterprise," said Jean Fairfax, director of the NAACP Legal Defense Fund.[23] Similar concerns were expressed by Dr. Samuel L. Meyers, former president of Bowie State College in Maryland and executive director of the National Association for Equal Opportunity in Higher Education.[24] In the long run, Meyers said, "it will be more costly to society if black schools disappear. Black colleges represent the best means we have to increase the flow of educated blacks out of disadvantaged positions and into productive roles in society. The pressures to let these institutions die are enormous. Blacks

---

[21] Wolters, *op. cit.*, p. 347.
[22] Daniel Payne College in Birmingham, Ala., Saints Junior College in Lexington, Miss., and Kittrell College in Kittrell, N.C.
[23] Quoted in the *Baltimore Sun*, June 27, 1979.
[24] Interview, Jan. 6, 1981.

and whites, though, would do well to develop a healthy skepticism about the so-called benefits that would bring."

Closing The 'Education Gap'

F OR DECADES black Americans fought to achieve integration in the nation's public schools.[25] In the last 25 years their efforts have resulted in numerous court decisions mandating educational equality. But lately desegregation has raised some difficult, perhaps unforeseen, questions for black educators. What happens if integration succeeds too well? And what would be the effect on black colleges if, by complying with the law to desegregate, their student bodies become predominantly white?

Ironically, black colleges, which came into existence because of racial segregation, have begun to feel the effects of a decade-old push by states and the federal government to dismantle dual public college systems for blacks and whites. The pressure is the result of a 1971 federal court ruling that found the government to be in violation of the 1964 Civil Rights Act for refusing to withhold funds from states with segregated schools. In ordering the Department of Health, Education and Welfare to begin enforcing the law, U.S. District Court Judge John H. Pratt of the District of Columbia noted the unique character of black colleges and instructed officials to do nothing that would threaten their well-being. Black institutions are heavily dependent on the federal government for much of their financial support. For some schools, federal aid makes up more than 30 percent of their annual budgets.

The federal government's current desegregation effort encourages black schools to adopt "other race" enrollment goals. It also requires them to upgrade their facilities to a point of comparability with those at white institutions. In addition, the government has notified states to discontinue "educationally unnecessary" programs. It is this requirement, in particular, that disturbs black college officials. The Department of Education maintains that eliminating duplicated programs at white and black schools located near one another is a vital step toward the enhancement of black colleges. But black educators believe that whatever duplicate courses their schools may offer are needed to help disadvantaged students master college-level work.

---

[25] See "Desegregation After 20 Years," *E.R.R.*, 1974 Vol. I, pp. 323-342.

Black public colleges historically have existed outside the purview of state education systems. However, many blacks now fear that pressure from the federal government will force state systems to absorb their schools and thus destroy their separate purpose and identity. It is argued that desegregating black colleges will make them "equal" to white schools. But supporters of black institutions disagree. "Black colleges don't perpetuate segregation or reward incompetence," Dr. Samuel L. Meyers told Editorial Reseach Reports. "It has been shown over the years that they offer the best way to bring blacks along in the education process free from the strains and cultural threats that exist on white campuses." Black colleges, Meyers said, "have the same right to exist as religious or military colleges do."

Nevertheless, economic hard times may make it difficult for state governments to continue supporting dual school systems. In fact, some states, including Maryland, North Carolina and Georgia, have already begun efforts to diversify student populations at neighboring white and black colleges by dividing programs between schools, inducing more whites to take courses at black institutions and vice versa. For example, at North Carolina A&T in Greensboro, students taking a new course in industrial engineering are 80 percent white; the schools' 5,500 students are 89 percent black. But black educators suggest such steps, while they may improve curricula, also have the effect of limiting attention to the special educational needs of blacks. If black students are pushed out of places in their own schools by incoming whites, they point out, any effort at balancing enrollment and upgrading facilities will have failed.

Title III: The Federal Assistance Lifeline

The problems black colleges face, wrote Harvard Law Professor Derrick Bell, have "been deposited on their collective doorstep not by racist enemies who for so long kept black schools separate and unequal, but by integrationists whose concern for the racial balance of each institution blinds them to educational realities."[26] Black colleges, their supporters contend, cannot and should not be judged on the same basis as their white couterparts. Just as their "special educational mission" should be taken into account when they are evaluated, so should their work be assisted by special federal programs.

If federal aid is a necessity for most colleges, it is an *absolute* necessity for black colleges. Without federal money, the majority of black schools would be in serious financial trouble and many probably would be forced to shut down. No doubt the

[26] Derrick Bell, "The Politics of Desegregation," *Change,* October 1979, p. 52.

Federal Aid to Higher Education, 1970-1979

(amounts in thousands)

Fiscal Year	All Colleges	Percent Change	Black Colleges	Percent Change	Black Colleges as Per-cent of Total
1970	$3,667,923	—	$121,999	—	3.3
1971	3,888,306	6.0	159,366	31.4	4.1
1972	4,637,637	19.3	242,226	52.0	5.2
1973	4,492,567	−3.1	239,673	−1.1	5.3
1974	4,852,814	8.0	266,896	11.4	5.5
1975	4,849,590	−0.7	233,144	−12.6	4.8
1976	5,380,022	10.9	264,754	13.6	4.9
1977	6,468,630	20.2	341,621	29.0	5.3
1978	8,826,700	36.5	361,297	5.8	4.1
1979	8,949,440	—	394,444	—	4.4

Source: Department of Education, 1980

most important conduit through which federal dollars flow to black institutions is Title III of the Higher Education Act of 1965. Title III is designed to assist small public and private schools maintain and develop academic programs. From the beginning, however, the bulk of Title III grants, nearly 60 percent annually, has gone to black colleges.

In 1978, HEW announced that it would review its Title III policy to determine if it should continue dispensing money to schools that could not survive without government help. Over half the nation's private black colleges were listed by HEW as "priority institutions for program review." The presidents of these schools rushed to meet with President Carter to stress the continuing need of their institutions. Afterwards, the White House praised the role of black colleges in American education, but did little to forestall HEW's Title III "reappraisals."

In 1979, the agency threatened to cut off $90 million in funds to North Carolina unless it revised plans to desegregate and improve its black colleges. The state has gone to court to halt the cutoff; the case has yet to be decided. In Georgia, officials at Albany State College have been warned that future federal aid to the black school hinges on its recruiting a student body that is 25 to 30 percent white. But meeting that goal, college officials say, would be an "impossible task." Similar challenges have been issued to schools in other states.

When it came time for Congress to renew authorization for Title III, a coalition of small, predominantly white colleges lobbied to have the legislation rewritten so as to better serve their needs. The House, on Nov. 7, 1979, reauthorized the old measure without making any significant changes. But the Senate began revising Title III in ways that would have eliminated many special considerations black schools have always received under the provisions. The United Negro College Fund (UNCF), which raises money for private black colleges, mobilized support for a compromise in the Senate version of Title III and succeeded in persuading reluctant lawmakers to restore some of the law's former language.

"The Senate passed a revised Title III, but it could have been a lot worse than it turned out," said Niles White, UNCF's government affairs director. "The initial Senate version would have cut as much as 80 percent of the money black colleges now receive."[27] Changes in the law gave white colleges greater access to federal aid. However, the new implementing regulations for Title III remain to be written. "We're waiting to see what those will be like," said White. "As of now, we really don't know how much they'll help or hurt us."

Prospects Under Reagan Administration

Against a backdrop of tight money and what some see as a diminishing sense of commitment to black higher education, black college officials say they face an increasingly difficult job in getting "our message" across in Washington. Hispanics, community and two-year colleges and the fiscally threatened small private schools[28] are all clamoring for a bigger portion of federal aid. With once-reliable sources of corporate support also starting to dry up, "black schools have to work harder than ever for dollars," said Niles White. "Of course, so does everybody else. The competiton is getting fierce."

The United Negro College Fund has recently turned to staging telethons as a means of raising funds. Using show business personalities to drum up contributions, UNCF collected $2.6 million in 1980. Although many educational groups express a reluctance to resort to this approach, the economic pinch could force them to try similar techniques to raise money.

In August, President Carter, making a strong pitch for the black vote, signed an executive order to expand the capacity of black colleges to gain federal assistance. The order required the secretary of education to work with the Office of Management and Budget and the heads of other government agencies to determine the extent to which black schools are "being unfairly excluded from aid programs" and to make the necessary improvements.[29]

---

[27] Interview Jan. 7, 1981. The Senate passed the reauthorization bill on June 24, 1980. It was signed by President Carter on Oct. 3, 1980.
[28] See "Future of Private Colleges," *E.R.R.*, 1976 Vol. I, pp. 305-322.
[29] Speaking at the White House, Aug. 8, 1980.

"The machinery to carry out Carter's order is all in place," White said. "But there's no telling whether Reagan will endorse the same policy or not. Republican administrations in the past have been very generous with black colleges. And we can only hope Reagan will do the same. Continuing Carter's initiative in one form or another would be a way for Reagan to show the black community that he's willing to help people who want to better themselves." But White concedes that other special interest groups are likely to exert a stronger claim on the new president's attention. "There's only so much money," he said. "And with the middle class now going after funds that poor people used to get, the next four years could be an uphill battle all the way."

The erosion of political backing for black higher education is an extension of the "uneven performance" of its Washington lobbying effort, contends journalist Ronald Taylor.[30] What Taylor and others would like to see is a Common Cause-type organization to represent the needs of black institutions. This kind of coalition might be successful in marshalling the same kind of support that existed for black higher education in the 1960s. Without such an infusion of new enthusiasm — and new dollars — there are many who believe that the future of black colleges could be bleak indeed.

[30] Ronald Taylor, "How To Win Friends and Influence Policy," *Change,* October 1979, p. 76.

Selected Bibliography

Books

Dillard, J. L., *Black English,* Random House, 1972.

Holmes, Barbara D., *Black Colleges and Title III: A Progress Report,* Banner Books International, 1978.

Locke, Alain, ed., *The New Negro* (revised edition), Atheneum, 1969.

Moore, William and Lonnie H. Wagstaff, *Black Educators in White Colleges,* Jossey-Bass, 1974.

Sowell, Thomas, *Black Education: Myths and Tragedies,* McKay, 1972.

Willie, Charles V. and Ronald R. Edmonds, *Black Colleges in America,* Teachers College Press, 1978.

Wolters, Raymond, *The New Negro on Campus: Black College Rebellions of the 1920s,* Princeton University Press, 1975.

Articles

Ebony, selected issues.

Henderson, Vivian W., "Blacks and Change in Higher Education," *Daedalus,* fall 1974.

The Chronicle of Higher Education, selected issues.

"The Education of Black Americans," *Change* (special issue), October 1979.

"The Future of the Black Colleges," *Daedalus* (special issue), summer 1971.

Reports and Studies

Carnegie Commission on Higher Education, "From Isolation to Mainstream: Problems of the Colleges Founded by Negroes," 1971.

Doermann, Humphrey, "Toward Equal Access," College Entrance Examination Board, 1978.

Editorial Research Reports: "Blacks on Campus," 1972 Vol. II, p. 665.

Peterson, Marvin W., Robert T. Blackburn, Zelda F. Gamson, Carlos H. Arce, Roselle W. Davenport and James R. Mingle, "Black Students on White Campuses: The Impact of Increased Black Enrollments," Institute for Social Research, 1979.

Smith, Cynthia J., "Advancing Equality of Opportunity: A Matter of Justice," Institute for the Study of Educational Policy, 1978.

Cover art by Staff Artist Robert Redding

THE BIG BUSINESS OF EMPLOYEE EDUCATION

by

Marc Leepson

THE BIG BUSINESS
OF EMPLOYEE EDUCATION

EMPLOYEE EDUCATION has become a big and growing business within American industry. Large and medium-sized companies across the country underwrite or actively sponsor a vast range of programs, from formal on-the-job training to reimbursement of employees for college tuition. Corporate employers willingly do so in the belief that better trained and educated workers tend to be happier — and more productive. There is another important reason, too. Rapid changes in such highly technical fields as computerization, information processing and telecommunications have all but forced competing businesses to help their employees stay abreast of the latest advances.

"The whole thing is wanting . . . employees to understand our business better, and consequently be more productive, be more helpful, answer the needs of our customers," said James C. Donohue, Xerox Corp.'s manager of education research and development. "As our business became more sophisticated, it became absolutely clear to us that if we were going to be successful, we had to train our people to do the kind of job we wanted them to do."[1] There also is criticism, by others in industry, that young men and women often come out of the American school system quite unprepared in such basics as reading, writing and arithmetic — and thus need remedial courses (see p. 74)

Because businesses have kept few records on their employee education activities, it is extremely difficult to determine the number of workers involved in educational programs and the amount of money businesses nationwide spend on them. What is known is that businesses are spending billions of dollars on employee education today and that millions of workers are taking advantage of the programs. The American Society for Training and Development, in Washington, D.C., estimates that private and public employers in this country spend about $30 billion to $40 billion annually on employee education. Alan P. Wagner, a professor of consumer sciences and retailing at Purdue University, comes up with a somewhat lower figure, about $10 billion, based on data from the National Center for Education Statistics, the U.S. Bureau of the Census and

---

[1] Interview, Nov. 14, 1980.

elsewhere. Although such estimates are "best guesses," Wagner said, he nevertheless felt confident that employer-sponsored, off-the-job education programs — excluding tuition aid — would train 12.7 million individuals in the private sector in 1980.[2]

A survey conducted by The Conference Board, a New York-based business research organization, and released in July 1977, found that 70 percent of 610 companies with 500 or more employees it surveyed offered in-house educational programs during working hours. About 89 percent provided either partial or total tuition compensation to employees. The survey found that 4.3 million employees (out of a total of 32 million) participated in some form of education program at work.

A separate survey taken for a committee of the Texas House of Representatives in May 1980 found that 74.4 percent of those Texas employers with 500 or more employees who responded to a questionnaire increased their budgets for training from 1979 to 1980. Some 60 percent of the respondents said they conducted 75 percent or more of their formal training on their premises. The survey found that "on-the-job training and/or formal in-house training are the methods organizations rely on most to improve basic knowledge, technical proficiency, supervisory and management skills, and personal development of their employees."[3]

There are four basic types of employee education and training programs:

Job-related training in which company personnel or outside instructors develop and conduct courses that usually are held on company premises. These courses typically are designed to teach employees the latest technological advances or other changes (such as government regulations) involving the job they perform.

Tuition-aid programs in which employees choose a course of study at an outside institution of higher learning and are reimbursed either fully or partially by their employer. Analysts say that, nationwide, companies pay about $500 million a year for employee tuition aid.

Other outside courses in which employees meet with others in their trade or profession and discuss problems of their work. The American Press Institute of Reston, Va., for example, sponsors about 15 seminars a year for sports editors, editorial writers, advertising managers, copy editors and other newspaper crafts. Newspaper employees meet at these seminars to discuss problems and solutions and to hear from panel-discussion leaders.

---

[2] Quoted in *Chronicle of Higher Education*, Sept. 22, 1980, p. 7.
[3] Texas House of Representatives, Select Committee on State Employee Productivity, "Employee Productivity and Performance, Private Sector Survey, Preliminary Analysis," May 1980, p. 16.

College-degree programs in which employees pursue not just a few job-related courses of study at a university or college but an entire curriculum leading to a degree. Classes often are held on company premises.

Seymour Lusterman, who supervised and wrote The Conference Board study, said of this wide-ranging commitment of American industry to education and training: "By almost any definition industry is, in fact, no less a segment of the nation's educational system than our colleges and universities, technical institutes, and other schools. It develops its own courses and curricula, employs faculty and non-teaching professional staff, carries on formal instructional activities, evaluates its programs and methods, and often does these in well-designed and equipped facilities that are devoted to them exclusively."[4]

AT&T's Pace-Setting Education Program

By far the largest employee education program is run by the nation's largest private employer, the American Telephone & Telegraph Co. "AT&T, the biggest private company in the world,[5] offers the largest education program in the U.S., spending about $1 billion a year in order to prepare its nearly one million employees," wrote *Financial World* contributing editor Stan Luxenberg. "It has hundreds of classrooms ranging from spare rooms in local Bell System offices to campus-style facilities.

AT&T trains its computer programmers, engineers, accountants, operators, and the thousands of managers needed to oversee the army of employees."[6] According to the July 26, 1980, issue of the American Society of Training

**AT&T Training
Dublin, Ohio**

and Development's *National Report*, "rough estimates" indicate

---

[4] Seymour Lusterman, "Education in Industry," The Conference Board, 1977, p. 3.
[5] AT&T is the parent company of Western Electric Co., Bell Laboratories and the 23 regional telephone companies that make up the Bell System. Since it is not an industrial corporation, AT&T is not listed among *Fortune* magazine's 500 largest corporations. But AT&T is the nation's largest corporation in terms of assets ($125 billion as of Nov. 30, 1980), employees (about 1,046,000) and net income ($5.8 billion in 1979).
[6] Stan Luxenberg, "AT&T and Citicorp: Prototypes in Job Training Among Large Corporations," *Phi Delta Kappan*, January 1980, p. 314.

Education-Training Programs
By Company Size

Company Size	Tuition Aid (after hours)	Other Outside (during hours)	Company Courses (after hours)	(during hours)
10,000 or more employees	97%*	90%	56%	96%
5,000 to 9,999	95	83	51	96
2,500 to 4,999	91	79	52	91
1,000 to 2,499	94	77	45	86
500 to 999	82	66	25	71
All companies	89	94	39	55

*Percentage of companies reporting programs in 1975 survey.

Source: Seymour Lusterman, "Education in Industry," The Conference Board, 1977

that the Bell System in 1980 ran about 12,000 employee training courses in 1,300 locations for some 20,000 to 30,000 employees per day. Those courses were taught with 13,000 to 15,000 trained staffers "at a cost of about $1.7 billion in 1980. These estimates are for training of one-half hour or more in length for the 1 million employees in management and non-management jobs in the Bell System," the report said.

What types of training programs are involved in this massive endeavor? "The training we do in the Bell System is very, very varied, all the way from training for pole climbers and operators to the training of engineers and managers," Harry A. Shoemaker, AT&T division manager for training and education, told Editorial Research Reports. Each of the Bell System's operating companies runs its own training organization, Shoemaker said. Most of those companies have one section, usually called the Human Resources Department, that is responsible for developing and delivering training. Other courses are developed by Bell System educators for use system-wide.

Bell of Pennsylvania and Diamond State Telephone, the public telecommunications utilities in Pennsylvania and Delaware, provide an example of a Bell operating company's individual educational program. The companies offer an array of educational programs, including courses in electronic data processing, engineering, management and marketing to their 32,000 employees. Bell of Pennsylvania and Diamond State also provide tuition aid for outside courses. The companies run their training programs through four departmental training groups, each of which has its own training center.

The highly structured AT&T programs have been evolving for almost two decades. The company began to develop the basis for today's widespread system in the mid-1960s. That effort intensified in the early 1970s. "At that time there was a bigger emphasis placed upon . . . efforts to produce standard courses in a number of areas," Shoemaker said.

There were several reasons for the new emphasis on training at that time. "One is more rapid technological change which has increased the range in the kinds of tasks we perform," Shoemaker explained. "The services we offer now are much more varied than they were during the time of the 'P.O.T.' — the plain old telephone. . . . Twenty or thirty years ago there was a very limited amount of variety of switching equipment. It consisted of electro-mechanical switches entirely. Now we have electronic switching, which is much more complex and requires much more training . . . more highly qualified people. The same things would be true of our means of transmission. At one time it was just telephone lines. Then it evolved to coaxial cable, then to microwave and satellite and fiber optics."

For its most complex training, AT&T has a number of special centers throughout the country. The main technical training center for managers is at Lisle, Ill. Its four branches are forecasting, engineering, business services and network operations (including circuitry and operator services). Courses are developed at the center, tested and then offered to the system's executives and engineers.

Elaborate Training at Xerox and IBM

Employee education has become an important part of the growing electronic data processing field. Xerox Corp., for example, operates a centralized facility near Leesburg, Va., that trains some 20,000 sales, service and management employees a year. Some 75,000 employees have passed through Xerox's International Center for Training and Management Development since it opened in June 1974. James C. Donohue, the center's manager of education research and development, said that Xerox spent about $160 million on training in 1979.

"Training is not an option. It's a necessity," Donohue said. "For every job in Xerox there is a training program. . . . Before you begin to perform as a salesman you come to Leesburg to have a basic training in sales. Or after you're hired from a technical school, you're sent to Leesburg to take the basic course in fixing Xerox machines."[7] The center also offers specialized courses, including a sales course on how to deal with the U.S. government. The center's training programs for

---

[7] Interview, Nov. 14, 1980.

company managers — which are not mandatory — include courses for middle, upper level and executive management. "In the course of your career with Xerox, you might come here . . . a dozen and a half times," Donohue said.

The center's 200 instructors are Xerox salesmen, technical representatives and managers. They typically are brought to Leesburg for periods of two to three years and then sent back to "the field," to be replaced by others fresh from their jobs. "This kind of keeps us in touch with the reality of what's going on out there," Donohue said. The center develops the training programs with a staff of 16 professional educators, training designers and educational technologists. Former students are given tests to determine the relationship between their job performances and what they learned at the center. "We've seen a dramatic increase in the productivity of salesmen since we've centralized training here," Donohue said. "The same thing with our technical people. . . ."

International Business Machines (IBM) also has an extensive education and training program. "IBM is a high-technology company," wrote Peter M. Dean, program manager of education development services. "Most of what it does involves new and more productive ways of doing things. As a result, the people who sell, install, maintain, and use its products must be continually educated. Consequently, education is a large and important part of the company. IBM educates both its own employees and those of its customers."[8]

IBM does not have a single, centralized training center. Instead, each of the company's divisions maps out its own training activities. The Data Processing Division, for example, has four educational departments. They are for (1) administrative, (2) management, (3) industry-specialized and (4) customer, sales and system engineering education. The last department alone operates five advanced education centers, as well as 12 other regional training centers. The largest is in Dallas, Texas. Summing up his company's commitment to training, Dean wrote: "Within the multinational corporation that is IBM, the education and training program will continue to change. The extent of this change cannot be foreseen, but it is clear that in-house education is vital to the continuing health of IBM."

Not all employee training programs are run by multinationals or other billion-dollar industries. Medium-sized industries across the country have training programs as well. One example is the Jet Propulsion Laboratory of Pasadena, Calif., which employs about 4,000 persons. The company provides employees

---

[8] Writing in *Phi Delta Kappan,* January 1980, p. 317.

with 16-hour, four-week courses on the psychology of leadership, an 18-hour course in effective negotiation, and other courses that can be applied toward college credit. The Dana Corp. offers one-week business and technical courses to employees at its Toledo, Ohio, headquarters.

Amtrak, the federally chartered railroad corporation, is setting up a national training center 70 miles east of Chicago in Donaldson, Ind. The $2.8 million center is expected to provide classes for up to 250 Amtrak employees. Amtrak operates a number of training centers for mechanical employees at facilities across the nation. But the new center, scheduled to open early this year, will be the first centralized facility for training station and on-board personnel.

The John Breunner Co., a 123-year-old retail home-furnishings chain of 14 stores in northern California, Arizona and Nevada, began a large-scale training program for its 1,600 employees several years ago. "The principle we followed," said the corporate training director, Bob Eddy, "was to work from the higher echelons of the store to the lower — partly because it is logical to start by trying to improve the skills of those who make the most important decisions, but also because the supervisors of those who are to be trained play vital roles in the process, which they must learn."[9] The heart of the training is a nine-day program spread out over a three-week period from early February to June. Nearly all of the company's higher- and middle-management personnel have taken the course in which they learn conceptual, human and technical skills.

College Credit Programs

EMPLOYEE EDUCATION is not limited to the training of personnel in skills directly related to their job performance. Many businesses also help employees gain college credit, and sometimes to complete degree programs. Of the college assistance programs, corporations are most likely to pay all or part of the employee's tuition for approved courses he or she has selected and attended at a nearby campus.

But sometimes employers set up college-credit courses, which usually are taught at the workplace. The American Council on Education's 1980 *National Guide to Education Credit for Training Programs* lists 95 private companies, trade unions, government bodies and other organizations — from the Ameri-

---

[9] Quoted by Lusterman, *op. cit.,* p. 73.

can Institute of Banking, to the Young Women's Christian Association of the U.S.A. — that offer employees about 1,000 of these courses. Less frequently, the cooperative program set up by a local college and an employer may offer an entire catalog of courses leading to an undergraduate degree.

Employees, employers and academic institutions all gain from these college programs. The companies get better-educated workers. The employees receive the chance to take college courses without sacrificing time (and income) at work. The colleges receive more students in an era of stagnant enrollments.[10] "It appears that more and more companies are making continuing education of this type a formal aspect of their human resources development programs," said Gregory B. Smith of the National Institute for Work and Learning, a policy-research organization based in Washington, D.C.[11]

Employer-College Course Cooperation

The move by businesses to cooperate with local colleges to run degree programs in the workplace has been termed "the trend of the future," by Donald W. Fletcher, associate dean for extended education at California State University and Colleges. "It makes sense to offer courses where students are," Fletcher said recently, "especially because of the energy situation."[12] Among the colleges and companies that have set up formal cooperative programs are:

Aetna Life and Casualty Co.	University of Hartford
Burroughs Corp.	Detroit College of Business
First Pennsylvania Bank, Philadelphia	Temple University
General Dynamics Corp., Groton, Conn.	University of New Haven
GMC Truck & Coach Div.	University of Detroit
Grumman Data Systems Corp.	C. W. Post Center of Long Island University
New England Telephone Co., Boston	Northeastern University
Pratt & Whitney Aircraft, East Hartford, Conn.	Manchester Community College
R. J. Reynolds Industries, Inc., Winston-Salem, N.C.	High Point College
Whirlpool Corp. and Chrysler Corp.	Central Michigan University's Institute for Personal Career Development

---

[10] In spite of the fact that the number of students in the traditional undergraduate age bracket has declined in recent years, the number of students enrolled at American colleges and universities rose 3.2 percent in the fall of 1980 compared to the fall of 1979. In preliminary statistics released by the National Center for Educational Statistics, enrollments in public and private universities were down 1.5 percent, but other four-year colleges reported a 4 percent increase. There was a 5.6 percent increase in the number of students enrolled in two-year institutions. See "College Admissions," *E.R.R.*, 1980 Vol. I, pp. 265-284.

[11] Interview, Nov. 13, 1980.

[12] Quoted in *Business Week*, Aug. 4, 1980, p. 76.

Overcoming 'Math Anxiety'

Does the company's new vice president suddenly feel overwhelmed and baffled by the reams of statistical analyses the computer is spewing out daily for him to digest? And does a junior-grade clerk 10 floors below feel equally frustrated, even threatened, by on-the-job problems of simple arithmetic — a subject he had managed to sluff off in school? If so, they both may suffer from "math anxiety," to use the currently fashionable term.

If it afflicts the business world, there should be a profitable remedy awaiting discovery. So reasoned Michael Nelson, a Boston psychiatrist, when he attended the Sloan School of Management at Massachusetts Institute of Technology. Upon graduation in 1977, he founded Mathematics Learning Co. and enlisted the help of a Harvard faculty member, Deborah Hughes Hallett, to devise a confidence-building course in math instruction.

This "math understanding" class was first offered the public in the fall of 1978 through Harvard's non-credit Life-Long Learning program. After initial success in academia, Dr. Nelson's small company began to sell its services to big corporations. Banks, insurance companies, General Electric and the Digital Corp. are among its clients.

As described by Jeanne McArthur, a Mathematics Learning director, trained math teachers set up classes to suit the needs of the employees, whether they are executives or clerk typists. These employee-students are all volunteers. Some attend class on company time, others on their own time, but all at the expense of their employer.

One of the most extensive programs is conducted by the Digital Equipment Corp., an international manufacturer of computer systems. At its plant in Maynard, Mass., company employees take courses leading to bachelor's degrees in business administration and master's degrees in electrical engineering and business administration. The teachers come from nearby Boston University, Clarke University and Worcester Polytechnic Institute. The University of New Hampshire also conducts an undergraduate degree program at the Digital plant in Merrimack, N.H. About 2,000 employees attend classes each year.

One reason for the popularity of on-site courses, aside from convenience, is that they tend to concentrate on technical and complex matters that employees need to know in their work. "With our hiring demands, the more people we develop in-house, the better," said Digital's manager of corporate management and employee development, Robert R. Clark.[13]

There has been some criticism, mostly by academics, of the

[13] Quoted in *Business Week, op. cit.,* p. 77.

on-site college degree programs. Some say that since industries lack many of the support functions of colleges, such as libraries and laboratories, the employee-student is shortchanged. Others say too much academic control, including the setting of admissions standards, is shifted from the university to the employer. Finally, some colleges considering such programs have found it difficult to adjust their programs to fit the needs of business.

"Many corporations have told me they have no desire to get into the higher-education business," said Allan W. Ostar, executive director of the American Association of State Colleges and Universities. "They would prefer to have the colleges and universities carry on activities of service training. But the problem is that the institutions have not been responsive to the more flexible needs of business and industry for time and places for education."[14]

James C. Donohue of Xerox Corp. told Editorial Research Reports that there is some fear in the academic community that industry is "beginning to take over" from the colleges. "The answer to that, of course, is no," he said. "I don't expect Harvard or Dartmouth or Yale to train someone specifically in how to manage, to sell, or fix Xerox machines. I do expect them to establish a foundation upon which we can build specifics. It's a cooperative effort as I see it, but there is some concern on the part of higher education with this continual growing of education that's being done by industry."

Donohue said that colleges and businesses have similar goals and should work more closely. "More and more colleges and universities, I think, should be talking with industry and finding out what kind of people they need," he said. "My answer is I don't need somebody that's straitjacketed into a particular technical course. I want someone that's kind of a generalist who is probably more adaptable in the long run to the kinds of things that we need within Xerox."

Extensive Tuition Aid From Businesses

Several surveys, including the Conference Board study, indicate that as many as 90 percent of the nation's large corporations provide tuition assistance for employees taking college courses away from the workplace. The American Society for Training and Development, in its *National Report* of Oct. 22, 1979, cited statistics showing that the average cost for each participant in a sample of 363 employer tuition-aid programs was $245.25. The average cost for the employee was less than $18 a course. The maximum allowance provided per employee ranged from $250 to $1,600. Nearly 60 percent of the employers

---

[14] Quoted in *Chronicle of Higher Education, op. cit.,* p. 7.

surveyed paid all tuition costs for employees. More than half the employers reported that women and minorities were using these programs "to a notable degree."

The Polaroid Corp. runs one of the most successful tuition-aid programs. An unusually high percentage of employees take advantage of the program, which pays the entire cost of approved courses at colleges, universities and technical schools. All employees working more than 20 hours a week are eligible. The company spends some $450,000 a year for these courses. They range from basic reading, writing and arithmetic to advanced work by employees seeking high positions in the company. The program also pays for trade and craft licensing certification as well as for degree programs.

During the 1977-78 academic year, some 6,000 Polaroid employees participated in more than one of the company's various training programs. Ten percent of the eligible work force participated in the tuition-assistance plan. "What is particularly interesting about Polaroid is the fact that a relatively high rate of participation is sustained in the presence of extensive opportunities for internal educational activity," said a report by the National Manpower Institute. "[B]oth management officials and plan participants attribute high participation rates to two major ... provisions: 1. 100% payment and 2. prepayment of tuition costs."[15]

College Degrees from General Motors

The nation's biggest manufacturer, General Motors, has a unique college-degree program. The company operates the General Motors Institute (GMI), the only fully accredited undergraduate college in the United States owned by a private corporation. The origins of GMI go back six decades. An employee-owned group, the Industrial Fellowship League, began sponsoring night classes in engineering and industrial administration in 1919 at a facility in Flint, Mich., called General Motors Institute. The company took over operations and became the institution's sole owner seven years later. General Motors built the first academic building on the school's present 43-acre site. Today, 2,200 students are enrolled at GMI on a cooperative basis. That is, they work 12 weeks in one of the 130 General Motors plants in the United States and Canada. Then they spend 12 weeks studying at GMI in Flint. The program lasts five years.

Lawrence Swanson, GMI administrative assistant to the president, said students from 44 states and Canada currently

[15] Kathleen Knox, "Polaroid Corporation's Tuition Assistance Plan: A Case Study," National Manpower Institute, September 1979, p. xv. The National Manpower Institute now is known as the National Institute of Work and Learning.

make up the student body. The students are recruited right out of high school, he explained, on the basis of academic performance and the usual college entrance requirements. GMI receives some 3,000 applications for 500 to 600 first-year positions annually. "Upon completion of the five-year program," Swanson said, "although they are not obligated to work for General Motors, and we are not obligated to offer them a job, about 96 percent of them do accept full-time employment with General Motors." About two-thirds of all GMI alumni now work for the company in some capacity, including GM President Elliott M. Estes of the class of 1938.

Relearning The Basics

C OLLEGE GRADUATES can't write reports; high school graduates can't read, spell, or write; and typists can't type more than 30 words a minute — and they all have poor vocabularies," the director of management development of a large company said recently. "Twelve years is a long time to spend in school and not come away with the basics. Maybe kids should come to us when they're eight years old."[16]

This businessman's complaint has been echoed by many others in business and government. The Conference Board said that 47 percent of the business leaders it surveyed found that their employees' education in writing, reading and arithmetic had been only "adequate" or "fair." Some 41 percent felt that employees' education in these basics was "inadequate" or "poor," and only 12 percent said it was "excellent" or "good."' The Conference Board estimated that in 1976 some 30,000 American workers participated in remedial courses during working hours and that 35 percent of the nation's companies with 10,000 or more employees provided such courses during or after work hours.

One highly visible offshoot of this "inadequate" preparation is the writing of business and government reports and forms. Incomprehensible writing has become a feature of many business letters, memoranda, loan agreements, insurance policies and other business documents. Overblown, unclear writing has become so prolific in government that the words "gobbledygook" and "bureaucratese" have been coined to describe it.

President Carter, in his first "fireside chat" on Feb. 2, 1977, promised to "cut down on government regulations . . . and make

---

[16] Quoted by Lusterman, *op. cit.*, p. 65.

sure that those that are written are in plain English for a change." Carter signed an executive order in March 1978 that called for all federal agencies to use "simple English." At least one agency, the U.S. Department of Transportation, took pains to teach its employees to simplify their writing. The culmination of that effort was a booklet that has been distributed to all department employees explaining clear writing techniques. The goal of the program is to "get rid of gobbledygook in letters and pay even more attention to pleasantness and helpfulness on the telephone."

Workplace Instruction in 'Plain Writing'

A number of companies across the nation have made a business out of teaching simplified language and communications. They include Siegel & Gale of New York City, the Pittsburgh Reading and Writing Center, Gunning-Mueller Clear Writing Institute of Santa Barbara, Calif., and the Center for Effective Communication in Chicago. "We get people who are swamped by their work because they need a whole hour to compose a simple, one-page letter," said Charlene Andolina, executive director of the Pittsburgh Reading and Writing Center, which sets up clear-writing seminars for other companies.[17]

Siegel & Gale's Language Training Group devises and conducts programs to teach business managers and other professionals how to prepare simpler, more efficient communications. These programs usually consist of three phases. First, writing samples of the company's personnel are studied by Siegel & Gale analysts. Then, a two- or three-day workshop is set up for about 20 employees. At the workshop, the participants analyze, discuss and rework their own writing samples. Finally, the analysts review samples of material the employees write after they return to their jobs. There are then informal meetings with individuals to work on particular problems.

The advice itself usually is simple: Use short sentences and simple words. Make each sentence count for one thought only. Use the active (rather than the passive) voice whenever possible. These suggestions coincide with Henry David Thoreau's advice in *Walden:* "Our life is frittered away by detail.... Simplify, simplify."

Judging by the popularity of training in business and industry in recent years, the immediate future should hold even greater growth. Tuition-aid programs, for example, were used by only about 63 percent of the major companies in 1957, compared to about 90 percent today.[18] One clear trend is an increasing use of training in medium-sized and smaller firms.

---

[17] Quoted in *The Wall Street Journal,* Aug. 28, 1980.
[18] Statistics cited by Ivan Charner, "Workers and Education: Tapping Tuition-Aid Benefits," National Manpower Institute, 1979.

Selected Bibliography

Books

Becker, Gary S., *Human Capital,* Columbia University Press, 1964.
Blaug, Mark, *An Introduction to the Economics of Education,* Penguin, 1972.
Craig, Robert L., ed., *Training and Development Handbook,* McGraw Hill, 1976.
Otto, Clavin P., and Rollin O. Glasser, *The Management of Training: A Handbook for Training and Development Personnel,* Addison-Wesley, 1970.
Wirtz, Willard, *The Boundless Resource,* The New Republic Book Co., 1975.

Articles

"Earning an Undergraduate Degree at the Plant," *Business Week,* Aug. 4, 1980.
Training and Development Journal and *National Report for Training and Development,* publications of the American Society for Training and Development, selected issues.
Watkins, Beverly T., " 'Post-Compulsory' Education by U.S. Companies May Be a $10-Billion Business," *Chronicle of Higher Education,* Sept. 22, 1980.
"Why Business Takes Education Into Own Hands," *U.S. News & World Report,* July 16, 1979.

Reports and Studies

American Council on Education, "National Guide to Education Credit for Training Programs," 1980, "Guide to the Evaluation of Educational Experiences in the Armed Forces," 3 vols., 1978.
Emanuel, Myron, *et al.,* "Corporate Economic Education Programs: An Evaluation and Appraisal," Financial Executives Research Foundation, 1979.
Editorial Research Reports: "America's Changing Work Ethic," 1979 Vol. II, p. 901; "Workers' Changing Expectations," 1980 Vol. II, p. 777.
General Motors Institute, "Engineering and Industrial Administration Programs, 1980-1981," May 1980.
Lusterman, Seymour, "Education in Industry," The Conference Board, 1977.
National Center for Education Statistics, "Digest of Education Statistics," May 1980, "Noncredit Activities in Institutions of Higher Learning," 1978.
National Institute for Work and Learning, "Training and Education in Industry," 1980; "Education and Training for Middle-Aged and Older Workers," 1980; "Worklife Education and Training and the Ordeal of Change," 1980.
Texas House of Representatives, Select Committee on State Employee Productivity, "Employee Productivity and Performance, Private Sector Survey, Preliminary Analysis," May 1980.
The Bureau of National Affairs, Inc., "Management Training and Development Programs," March 1977; "Training Programs and Tuition Aid Plans," October 1978.

Cover illustration by Staff Artist Robert Redding

76

FOREIGN LANGUAGES: TONGUE-TIED AMERICANS

by

Veronica Huang Li

**Sept. 19
1 9 8 0**

FOREIGN LANGUAGES:
TONGUE-TIED AMERICANS

THE IMAGE of the provincial American is no longer funny; it has become a national concern. A number of prominent politicians, diplomats and educators are attributing some of the country's international woes to Americans' ignorance of the cultures and languages of other peoples. They deplore the nation's deficiency in foreign language training and suggest that perhaps the Vietnam War, the seizure of American hostages in Iran and other incidents could have been avoided if Americans had a better understanding of the world. This has sparked a national movement to expand foreign language training in U.S. schools and universities.

In a report published late last year, the President's Commission on Foreign Language and International Studies concluded that "Americans' incompetence in foreign languages is nothing short of scandalous, and it is becoming worse." [1] Foreign language training is vital to "the nation's security," the commission said. "At a time when the resurgent forces of nationalism and of ethnic and linguistic consciousness so directly affect global realities," it stated, "the United States requires far more reliable capacities to communicate with its allies, analyze the behavior of potential adversaries, and earn the trust and the sympathies of the uncommitted. Yet there is a widening gap between these needs and the American competence to understand and deal successfully with other peoples in a world of flux."

The commission said foreign language training also would be useful in improving America's balance of trade. At a time of growing global competition, the commission said, American businessmen need to rally all the advantages they can summon, including the ability to speak the customer's tongue (see p. 81).

Because of the large number of immigrants coming to the United States, bilingualism is no longer a rarity but a way of life in many parts of the country. The U.S. Immigration

---

[1] President's Commission on Foreign Language and International Studies, "Strength Through Wisdom, A Critique of U.S. Capacity," November 1979. The commission was established in 1978 to carry out the stipulations of the 1975 Helsinki Accords. The 33 nations signing the accords agreed to respect human rights, allow freer exchanges and travel by each nation's citizens and to "encourage the study of foreign language and civilization as an important means of expanding communication among peoples."

and Naturalization Service reports that in 1978, the latest year for which statistics are available, 601,000 immigrants entered the country. One-third of those immigrants were Spanish-speaking.

Hispanics are fast becoming the nation's largest ethnic group. High birth rates and the influx of new arrivals from Cuba and other Latin American countries have boosted the Hispanic population to 20 million, according to Rodolfo Balli Sanchez, executive director of the National Coalition of Hispanic Mental Health and Human Services Organizations. Many live in close-knit neighborhoods where the culture and language of their ancestors are retained. Asians are another fast growing population group in the United States. In 1978, the latest year for which statistics are available, 88,500 Vietnamese arrived in the United States. A total of 250,000 Asian immigrants came to America that year, according to the U.S. Immigration and Naturalization Service.

Inadequacies in Diplomacy and in Business

The state of foreign language training in the United States is perhaps most evident in the U.S. diplomatic corps. The General Accounting Office reported last spring that in the U.S. Foreign Service, only 71 percent of the posts labeled "language essential" are filled by qualified persons. Many U.S. consular officials have to limit local contacts to a small circle of English-speaking natives. Although interpreters are available, some local nationals are reluctant to deal through them. Embassy staff members admit that it is difficult to get the true meaning of a conversation when working through a translator.[2] This is a problem when collecting intelligence, conducting negotiations and dealing with host government officials on behalf of American citizens.

In crisis situations, the difference can be between life and death. U.S. Ambassador Diego Asencio, who comes from a Spanish-speaking family in Newark, N.J., believes he owes his life to his language ability. Asencio was among 30 officials taken hostage by terrorists in Bogota, Colombia, last March. Released after two months in captivity, Asencio told a reporter: "I believe my ability to communicate with my captors — on various levels — was crucial in saving my life."[3]

Others have been less fortunate. Adolph Dubs, the U.S. ambassador to Afghanistan, was killed after being abducted by terrorists in February 1979. Observers blamed the tragedy partly on U.S. embassy officials' inability to bargain fluently

---

[2] General Accounting Office, "More Competence in Foreign Languages Needed by Federal Personnel Working Overseas," April 15, 1980, p. 16.
[3] Interview with Roger Langley of the Washington Writers Syndicate, May 14, 1980.

Opinions About Foreign Language Study

Percent who agree that foreign language should be:

Offered in elementary school	76
Required in elementary school	42
Offered in high school	92
Required in high school	47
Required for college admission	38
Required for college graduation	40

Source: Telephone opinion poll conducted by the Survey Research Center, University of Michigan, 1979.

in any of the Afghan languages or to stop Afghan security aides from staging a raid that resulted in Dubs' death. At the time the U.S. embassy in Iran was seized, on Nov. 4, 1979, only three of the Americans taken hostage were proficient in Farsi, the language spoken by most Iranians.

The language deficiency is as glaring in the business sector as it is in the diplomatic community. The findings of the President's Commission on Foreign Language and International Studies provided some insight into the U.S. trade deficit with Japan. It cited estimates of 10,000 English-speaking Japanese businessmen in the United States and only a handful of Japanese-speaking American businessmen in Japan. "In that situation who do you think sells more?" asks Rep. Paul Simon, D-Ill., in his book *The Tongue-Tied American,* which will be published later this year.

While Japanese businessmen follow the motto, "The most important language is that of my customer," American companies traditionally have ignored foreign language training. The comment of one businessman typifies this attitude: "We send our people overseas to do a job. We are concerned only that they have the technical skill, because the people they will be working with overseas all speak English." [4] To cope with this problem, many U.S. companies doing business abroad are replacing Americans with local employees who have a command of English. U.S. multinationals sometimes track foreign students in the United States and offer them jobs immediately upon graduation.

Samuel Hayden, managing director of the Council of the Americas, a business association of more than 200 corporations having investments in Latin America, believes U.S. businessmen cannot afford to lose business opportunities because of language deficiency. He maintains that U.S. corporations and business schools have a shared responsibility to stress the utility of foreign languages as tools for doing business. "Business diplomacy is a fact of international commerce," he wrote re-

[4] Quoted by Marianne Inman, "Language in Education: Theory and Practice," Center for Applied Linguistics, May 1978, p. 1.

Foreign Language Enrollments in Public Secondary Schools

	1970	1974	1976*
Total enrollment	18,407,000	20,990,000	21,117,000
Foreign language enrollment	4,570,000	4,038,000	3,784,000
Percent of total	24.8	19.2	17.9

*Latest year for which statistics are available.
Source: American Council on the Teaching of Foreign Languages

cently. "Executives regularly communicate both socially and professionally with government officials abroad. In representing both their companies and the United States, there are great opportunities for goodwill ambassadorial relations. Many of the top executives who operate at these levels are in fact fluent in foreign language. But as the next cadre of executives do not have extensive experience abroad, where will these commercial ambassadors come from?"[5]

Language Enrollment Decline in Schools

The State Department, the International Communication Agency, the Department of Defense and other government agencies concerned with international affairs believe that declining foreign language enrollments in U.S. schools will lower the quality of new recruits and increase their language training costs.[6] Rep. Simon, who recently examined the educational systems of 74 countries, said that "none can compare with the United States in neglect of foreign languages."[7] The presidential commission found that:

Only 8 percent of American universities now require a foreign language for admission, compared with 34 percent in 1966.
Only 15 percent of high school students now study a foreign language, down from 24 percent in 1965.
Only one out of 20 public high school students studies French, German or Russian beyond the second year. Four years is considered a minimum for achieving usable language competence.

There have been some minor exceptions to this downward trend. The General Accounting Office reported that from 1960 to 1974, enrollment in Chinese language programs in American universities increased to 10,616 from 1,763, and in Japanese to 9,604 from 1,539. But the entire category of the less-commonly-taught languages (other than English, French, German,

---

[5] Samuel Hayden, "Foreign Languages, International Studies, and Business (A Dubious Savior)," *The Annals of the American Academy of Political and Social Science,* May 1980, p. 147.
[6] President's Commission on Foreign Language and International Studies, op. cit., p. 7. The United States currently spends more than $100 million annually on language training for government employees.
[7] Paul Simon, "The U.S. Crisis in Foreign Languages," *The Annals of the American Academy of Political and Social Science,* May 1980, p. 35.

Italian, Latin and Spanish) accounts for only 1 percent of the language class registrations in the nation's secondary schools and 10.2 percent in its colleges. Yet these are the languages spoken by over 80 percent of the world's population, and several of them have for many years been classified by the State Department as "strategic" or "critical" to U.S. interests.

But statistics do not tell all. Educators frequently complain that language requirements in U.S. schools are measured in years and semester hours rather than the standard achieved. "[W]e have no evidence that the quality of language instruction, or the levels of competence achieved by students were higher in 1966, when 89 percent of the colleges had requirements, than they are today," said Richard Brod of the Modern Language Association. "Indeed there is reason to think that the revolt against them that began in 1968 was fueled by a widespread realization that requirements guaranteed nothing except bodies in the classroom for a fixed period of time. Whether anyone learned anything during that period of time was not at issue." [8]

Student Apathy Toward Language Training

Reasons for apathy toward language study are many: poor teaching, lack of a national yardstick for proficiency and limited usage and employment opportunities. Underlying all these, many experts say, is an ethnocentric attitude that regards foreign language training as unessential and encourages immigrants to abandon their roots and plunge into the American melting pot.

Some see American parochialism as just an addition to the education system's catalog of sins. If public schools cannot teach Johnny to read English, how can they teach him French? Educators identify the lack of a national proficiency standard for English and other languages as a significant shortcoming. A goal must be set before students can attain it, they say.

[8] Letter from Brod to Rep. Paul Simon, May 16, 1980. The Modern Language Association, based in New York City, promotes literary and linguistic study and does research on foreign language instruction in U.S. schools. It was founded in 1883 and now has 30,000 members.

Dull pedagogy and irrelevance are frequently mentioned as other reasons behind this revolt. Foreign language training is suffering a credibility gap, said James Frith, dean of the School of Language Studies of the U.S. Foreign Service Institute. "Students who had A's in their language courses go overseas and they find themselves unable to understand what people are saying. They feel ripped off by language teachers." [9]

The emphasis on teaching literature rather than the spoken language is seen as one of the culprits. A foreign language major may be well-versed in, say, Spanish literature but incapable of buying a train ticket in Mexico. Dr. H. A. Merklein, who was employed by the International Institute of the University of Dallas to improve the linguistic abilities of graduate business administration students, discovered that most foreign language majors with a B.A. degree are not skillful enough to use their foreign language as a working tool. Many graduates cannot sit at a negotiating table to discuss contracts and some cannot even carry on a conversation, he said. [10]

If the proficiency of college language majors is low, that of the ordinary high school teacher is likely to be lower. A 1967 Harvard study showed that college seniors who were foreign language majors scored higher in linguistic skills than did teachers at language institutes. [11]

Failure to stimulate student interest in areas beyond the American shoreline also accounts for the language deficiency. In a recent study of schoolchildren's knowledge and perceptions of other nations, over 40 percent of the 12th graders queried could not locate Egypt, and over 20 percent could not find France or China. At the college level, less than 5 percent of prospective teachers take any courses relating to international affairs or foreign peoples as part of their professional education, according to Rose Lee Hayden, head of the U.S. Government Exchanges Policy and Coordination Division of the International Communication Agency. [12]

Cutbacks in Support for Foreign Study

Financial cutbacks in the 1970s contributed to the decline in foreign language study. Federally financed foreign language and international study fellowships declined to 828 in 1978 from a peak of 2,557 in 1969. During the same period, federal expenditures for university foreign affairs research dropped to

---

[9] Interview, Aug. 1, 1980.
[10] H. A. Merklein, "Multinational Corporate Perceptions of an International M.B.A. Degree," *Association of Departments of Foreign Languages Bulletin,* May 1975.
[11] "The Foreign Language Attainments of Language Majors in the Senior Year: A Survey Conducted in U.S. Colleges and Universities." The study was published by the Harvard University Printing Office, 1967.
[12] Speech delivered May 17, 1980, at Wayne State University.

$8.5 million from $20.3 million. The Ford Foundation now contributes only $3 million-$4 million a year for advanced training and research in international affairs, down from $27 million annually in the early 1960s.

The network of international studies centers built by foundations and universities in the postwar era is now in jeopardy. Programs such as the East Asian Studies Center at the University of Berkeley, the African Studies Center at Michigan State University and the Latin American Studies Center at San Diego State University are struggling to survive.

The plight of college graduates with language degrees is also discouraging. Most employers place little value on the language competence of job applicants, a 1979 Rand Corporation report suggests. It found that the market demand for international specialists remains small, absorbing about one-fourth to one-third of the available supply.[13] Government agencies employ about 6 percent of those receiving doctoral degrees in international affairs each year and no more than 9 percent of the available master's degrees in this field. Business and industry hire about 15 percent of those receiving graduate degrees in international studies. This situation does not apply across the board, of course. Specialists in Africa and the Middle East, for example, enjoy much better job prospects. Interdisciplinary students, such as those combining language training and economics, are also highly marketable.

In the State Department and other government agencies concerned with international relations, language skills are not always regarded as an asset on the promotion ladder. In fact, some disincentives to learn the less commonly used languages exist.[14] In many agencies, if a person has language expertise, he is expected to serve a good portion of his time in countries where that language predominates. This discourages some people from seeking training in languages that are used in few geographic areas. These areas are often hardship posts shunned by many career diplomats.

While the recommendations of the presidential commission met with wide approval from those who advocate more foreign language training, general resistance to reform is strong. Many Americans cling to the belief that English is sufficient in the conduct of international affairs. After all, English is spoken by more people — approximately 400 million — than any tongue except Mandarin Chinese. It has displaced French as the lan-

---

[13] "Foreign Language and International Studies Specialists: The Marketplace and National Policy," Rand Corporation, September 1979, p. 57.
[14] "More Competence in Foreign Languages Needed by Federal Personnel Working Overseas," *op. cit.*, p. 26.

guage of diplomacy and German as the language of science. Moreover, it reigns supreme as the language of international business. Others argue that foreign language is an educational frill that is expendable, particularly in the presence of budgetary cutbacks and more pressing problems such as teaching youngsters to master basic reading, writing and arithmetic.

Linguists counter with the theory that foreign language training helps Johnny read English. A Ph.D. dissertation at the University of Idaho concluded that two or more years of high school foreign language study had a "significant positive effect" on students' achievement in English.[15] In recent years, dozens of elementary schools across the nation have introduced Latin courses to help students who read English below grade level. The basic idea is to teach Latin word roots, prefixes and suffixes to improve students' English vocabulary. Educators generally are pleased with the results of such experiments. In Los Angeles, for example, Latin-trained students scored as much as a year ahead of other students on English achievement tests.[16] Los Angeles teachers also have found Latin useful in helping Spanish-speaking students learn English. "We show how the Romance languages, especially Spanish, go all the way back to the ancient Romans," said Albert Baca, the head of the program. "It gives students a sense of pride." [17]

Bilingualism and American Society

MULTILINGUALISM has taken a roller-coaster course in U.S. history. "It comes in cycles," said Josue Gonzalez, director of the U.S. Office of Bilingual Education and Minority Languages Affairs, depending on how the country feels about itself at the time.[18] Often economic, domestic or international events set the pendulum in motion.

America started out as a land of many languages. Instances of non-English and bilingual education were not uncommon in 18th- and 19th century America. Before the Civil War, German-English public schools existed in several states. There were also French-English programs in Louisiana and Spanish-English programs in the Territory of New Mexico. Norwegian, Czech, Italian, Polish and Dutch also were occasionally taught

---

[15] Terry Bastian, "An Investigation into the Effects of Second Language Learning on Achievement in English," July 1979.
[16] Reported in *Newsweek*, Nov. 12, 1979, p. 126.
[17] Quoted in *The Wall Street Journal*, Oct. 3, 1979.
[18] Interview, July 31, 1980.

in American public schools during this period. In addition, bilingual instruction flourished in many private (chiefly church) schools set up for immigrant children from Eastern and Southern Europe.[19]

Many bilingual and foreign language schools disappeared in the wave of nationalism, anti-Catholicism and xenophobia that swept the United States in the late 1800s and early 1900s. Most Americans at the time accepted the myth of America as a "melting pot" — a country where diverse ethnic and religious groups soon blended into a homogeneous mass. This assimilationist position was sanctioned at the highest levels of government. Theodore Roosevelt, in his book *The Foes of Our Household* (1917), wrote that "any man who comes here ... must adopt the institutions of the United States, and therefore he must adopt the language which is now the native tongue of our people.... It would not be merely a misfortune but a crime to perpetuate differences of language in this country."

The isolationist sentiment that took hold in the United States after World War I contributed to a further decline of foreign language instruction. Insulated from the rest of the world by oceans, Americans felt little need to communicate with foreigners. World War II drew the United States out of its isolationism. Americans became concerned about their ignorance of regions hitherto neglected. In 1942, the American Council of Learned Societies, National Research Council and others formed an Ethnogeographic Board to provide the armed forces and other government agencies with knowledge on foreign regions during the war years.

Modest expansion of these activities continued in the postwar era. But because the United States enjoyed unquestioned global leadership at the time, the need to talk to others on an equal footing was not urgent. There were only a few new foreign area programs, largely concentrated in graduate programs at several major universities.[20] Oriented primarily to East Asia and the Soviet Union, the content of these programs reflected the shift in American international interests. Foundations, especially the Carnegie Corporation and Ford Foundation, provided much of the financial resources for these programs.

Language Resurgence in Post-Sputnik Era

In 1957, Russia's launching of Sputnik, the world's first artificial satellite, triggered an upswing in foreign-language study. As U.S. leaders examined the Soviet education system for clues to Russian superiority in space, they discovered the Soviet

---

[19] See Theodore Andersson and Mildred Boyer, *Bilingual Schooling in the United States,* Vol. I (1970), pp. 17-40.

[20] Robert E. Ward and Bryce Wood, "Foreign Area Studies and the Social Science Research Council," Social Science Research Council, Vol. 28, No. 4, December 1974.

Army Teaching: A Better Way?

The Army Specialized Training Program, born in the midst of World War II, broke with traditional classroom teaching of foreign languages. Rather than emphasizing grammar, the Army stressed vocabulary, especially idiomatic speech, and everyday customs of the country. This approach, a wartime act of necessity, only dimly influenced postwar teaching in the classrooms but was adapted especially to the language training offered by commercial firms.

About 4,000 persons from all branches of the military service and the intelligence community annually receive training at the army's Foreign Language Center in Monterey, Calif. Its intensive nine-month course is claimed to be equivalent to six years of high school and college instruction. About 100,000 government workers benefit from the schools' non-resident programs, which include short language and orientation courses to prepare military officers and their dependents for overseas assignments.

emphasis on science, mathematics and foreign languages. Congress in 1958 passed the National Defense Education Act to support the study of these subjects in American schools.

The act sought to "meet the present education emergency" by providing federal financial assistance to individuals and states "in order to insure trained manpower of sufficient quality and quantity to meet the national defense needs." Title VI of the act authorized grants to institutions of higher learning to (1) establish and operate centers to teach any needed modern foreign language for which adequate instruction is not readily available and (2) support instruction in other fields needed to fully understand the geographic areas where the language is commonly used. A network of international studies centers mushroomed at American universities. Eighty of these centers remain in existence today, down from a peak number of 106 a decade ago.

The act designated five languages for priority funding: Arabic, Chinese, Hindustani, Portuguese and Russian. Later, 18 other languages, including Korean, Hebrew, Indonesian and Swahili, were designated second priority. Since its inception, Title VI has received a total of $260 million in funding; the 1980 appropriations were $17 million.

The Fulbright-Hays Act of 1961 broadened the president's authority to finance the costs of sending Americans abroad and bringing foreigners to the United States for educational, scientific and cultural purposes. The Fulbright Scholarships, named after Sen. J. William Fulbright, D-Ark. (1945-74), are part of this program. So far, Fulbright-Hays Act funds have amounted to $38 million.

Private foundations also contributed large sums of money to language training. Funds from the Carnegie, Rockefeller, Ford, Sloan, New World foundations and others poured into the development of innovative teaching methods. One such method, the "New Key," emphasized oral skills and reading comprehension rather than grammar. This method dominated foreign language training for a decade. New textbooks replete with dialogues and pattern practice drills quickly superseded the older grammar books. Tapes of native speakers reciting the dialogues and drills became indispensable, and millions of students listened to them in language laboratories, which sprang up everywhere. By 1962, some 6,000 high schools had language laboratories.[21] Similar facilities were set up in some elementary schools. Prior to World War II, only a few grade schools offered foreign languages, but by 1964, an estimated two million children were learning other languages.

Vietnam War Aftermath: 'Inward Looking'

By the late 1960s, however, interest in language training had again declined. Observers have pointed to the Vietnam War as one of several factors that spurred the decline. "The Vietnam War left a come-home, leave-foreigners alone legacy, especially among the young," said a *Washington Post* editorial on the recommendations of the President's Commission on Foreign Language *(see p. 79).*[22] The student "revolt" of the late 1960s also had an effect. Students demanded a bigger voice in the courses being offered and made "relevance" their guide and catchword. Foreign language courses tended to be declared irrelevant. Many colleges yielded to such demands and scrapped language requirements altogether. Some educators argued that it was too late to start teaching a foreign language at the college level.

Foreign language enrollment in secondary and elementary schools also went downhill rapidly. From 1968 to 1976, language registrations in public secondary schools dropped from 4.8 to 3.8 million, although total school population increased. Current statistics on language instruction in elementary schools are nonexistent, an indication of the paucity of language courses at that level.

Reduced federal funding paralleled the American withdrawal from Vietnam and the national reassessment of America's international role. In fiscal year 1971, the Nixon administration asked Congress to provide only one-third of the sum requested in the previous year for Title VI of the National Defense Education Act, and in 1974 proposed no funds at all. However,

---

[21] Mary H. Jackson, "Foreign Languages — Yesterday, Today and Tomorrow," booklet published by the National Education Association, 1975.
[22] *The Washington Post*, Nov. 10, 1979.

Congress appropriated $11.3 million that year and funding has since levelled at around $17 million. The budget for the Fulbright scholarships also dropped sharply after 1969 and only gradually was returned to the original level of about $3 million annually. The costs of doing research abroad, however, have increased substantially in recent years.

Recommendations and Outlook

TO HALT the decline in language training, the President's Commission on Foreign Language and International Studies made more than 60 recommendations estimated to cost $180 million to implement. Some modest steps have been taken so far. Secretary of Education Shirley M. Hufstedler has announced her commitment to foreign language education. "What is needed," she said, "is a conscious effort to overhaul our [language] educational experience: to take a fresh look at existing curricular offerings, at textbooks, at syllabi, at the quality of language teaching, and indeed, at the capacities of teachers." [23]

To further these goals, Hufstedler upgraded the Division of International Education to the status of Office of International Education, giving it more clout in bureaucratic politics. A national council funded by private foundations has been established to follow up on the commission's recommendations, and a number of states have formed committees to look into the problem.

In Congress, the commission's report has spawned several bills to expand language training programs. The most comprehensive is the "International Education Programs," which is offered as Title VI of a proposed set of amendments to the existing Higher Education Act. If enacted into law, this title would replace Title VI of the National Defense Education Act, which now is seen as inadequate. The proposed program includes $7.5 million in grants to programs promoting business participation in international education. Its purpose is to restore competitiveness to American products by sensitizing U.S. businessmen to foreign cultures and languages. The outlook for passage of the International Education Programs bill still is in doubt.

On June 13, Rep. Simon introduced a bill to provide per capita grants to reimburse elementary schools and institutions

---

[23] Shirley M. Hufstedler, "A World in Transition," *Educating for the World View,* The Council on Learning, p. 9.

of higher education for part of the costs of providing foreign language instruction. Simon also has sponsored an amendment to the proposed Foreign Service Act. If enacted the amendment would designate one U.S. embassy in a non-English-speaking country as a "model foreign language competence post," meaning all U.S. personnel there would have minimum competence in the native tongue.[24]

A bill introduced by Rep. Leon Panetta, D-Calif., and now pending before the House Education and Labor Committee, would require the secretary of education to establish a program of grants to universities to promote enrollment in foreign language and international studies. Another Panetta bill, passed by the House in June, seeks to make more effective use of returned Peace Corps volunteers who are familiar with foreign languages and cultures.

Efforts to Upgrade Quality of Instruction

More important than large enrollments, however, is the quality of instruction. The presidential commission recommended new teaching methods and materials and the establishment of a nationwide proficiency standard. The commission suggested the creation of 15 to 20 regional centers to upgrade language competency and cultural awareness among teachers. These centers would design teaching materials, curricula and language-testing tools, provide instruction in language methodology for prospective teachers, and train teachers of literature to teach the spoken language more effectively.

Mary Jackson, in a report published by the National Education Association in 1975, noted that the enrollment of corporation executives in language schools has increased rapidly in recent years. She said that courses such as international trade and law taught in a foreign language were highly successful. "The message seems obvious," Jackson wrote. "If foreign language courses are relevant, students will enroll in them. . . . The future should see more emphasis on courses that can assist those who plan for careers involving foreign languages — courses emphasizing translating, interpreting, travel and tourism, international law, international trade, and so on." [25]

The movement to establish a national language proficiency standard also is gaining momentum. A language task force sponsored by the Modern Language Association assembled language specialists from all over the nation in 1978 to focus on this need. One starting point is the "testing kit" of the

---

[24] The act is intended to help the Foreign Service attract and retain high-quality personnel by reorganizing its structure and improving employee benefits. The House version of the bill passed Sept. 8, the Senate version on Sept. 15.
[25] Mary Jackson, *op. cit.*

Foreign Service Institute, the training school in Arlington, Va., for Foreign Service officers. Educators participating in a workshop testing the FSI kit were impressed by the accuracy of the techniques in gauging a student's language skills, and recommended using it on college campuses.[26]

"What is needed is a conscious effort to overhaul our [language] educational experience: to take a fresh look at existing curricular offerings . . . at the quality of language teaching and at the capacities of teachers."

—Secretary of Education
Shirley M. Hufstedler

Many educators believe that students' language competence can improve by leaps and bounds if they are submerged in the culture in which the language is used. Since not everybody can live abroad to experience this kind of "cultural immersion," innovative language schools simulate foreign environments to make it possible. The "total immersion" courses of the Berlitz Schools of Languages, for example, plunge a student into a language nine hours a day, five days a week for a period of two to six weeks. The foreign language is the only thing he hears during the day, including lunch. In the evening, he takes home cassettes and other materials to work with. At the end of two weeks, the average student can handle basic, everyday conversation in the foreign language. Berlitz has 200 centers located in 22 countries.

The presidential commission also believes that cultural exchanges can take place at home. It proposed two-way bilingual programs to encourage interaction between native English speakers and immigrants who speak a foreign language. It also called on state authorities to support the thousands of ethnic language schools operated by minority groups.

Obstacles for Bilingual Education Program

Bilingual education faces many obstacles. Since the enactment of the Bilingual Education Act in 1968,[27] many bilingual programs have sprung up, but in recent years some communities

---

[26] James R. Frith, "Testing the FSI Testing Kit," *Association of Departments of Foreign Languages Bulletin*, Vol. 11, No. 2, Nov. 1979, pp. 12-14. The FSI test rates students on a scale of one to five; three stands for minimum professional proficiency while five represents the competence of a native speaker.

[27] See "Bilingual Education," *E.R.R.*, 1977 Vol. II, pp. 619-636.

Handicap in Negotiations

American business negotiators often are handicapped by their inability to understand the other side's language. Even when the negotiation is conducted in English, the foreign negotiators sometimes break into a discussion in their native tongue, leaving the Americans in the dark. When interpreters are available, the foreigners who understand English can take advantage of the time of translation to calculate a response. This gives them an edge, which may be crucial in tough bargaining sessions.

In his forthcoming book *The Tongue-Tied American*, Rep. Paul Simon wrote about such frustrations. While serving as a delegate to the United Nations session on disarmament in 1978, Simon noted the Russians' fluency in English gave them an advantage. "It gives the opposition in any such dialogue additional time to prepare for the proper reply," Simon wrote. "I wish I could enter a vigorous debate on the floor of the House with those kinds of odds stacked in my favor," he added.

have shown signs of a backlash. Resentment is growing against the enormous costs and the inefficiency of some programs due to a lack of qualified teachers. The bilingual regulations recently proposed by the Department of Education further fueled the dispute. The rules would require public schools to offer classes taught in a foreign language to students who are less skilled in English, but who would move to regular classes as their English improved. The department has invited public comment on the proposed rules and, so far, opposition has been strong. Some educators see the proposed requirement as an encroachment on the schools' rights.

The current Bilingual Education Act does not make the establishment of bilingual programs mandatory. It encourages their development by means of grant provisions. In 1974, the Supreme Court reaffirmed the special needs of language-minority children. In a unanimous decision, the court ruled that public schools were required by federal law to take "positive action" to help children who do not speak English.

The language decline is showing signs of bottoming out. A 1979 survey conducted by the University of Michigan Research Center indicated that while most Americans cannot speak any language but English, half of those surveyed wish they could.[28] Three-quarters of those surveyed believed foreign languages should be taught in elementary schools, although 70 percent of them never had the opportunity to study a foreign language in school.

In addition to international pressures, changing demography within the United States is forcing Americans to confront the language issue. In Texas, for instance, about 70,000 elementary

---

[28] The study was ordered by the President's Commission on Foreign Language and International Studies.

How Well Government Agencies Are Filling Language Designated Positions Overseas

Agency	Authorized	Filled	Filled at required proficiency level
Department of Defense*	13,597	10,752	7,333
Department of State	1,320	1,216	858
Agency for International Development	687	541	394
International Communication Agency	421	396	276
Drug Enforcement Administration	204	194	189
Internal Revenue Service	168	168	168
Animal and Plant Health Inspection Service	112	90	73
Peace Corps	72	64	56
Foreign Agricultural Service	60	59	21
Executive Office of U.S. Attorneys	20	19	19
Federal Bureau of Investigation	19	19	17
Center for Disease Control	18	15	14
U.S. Travel Service	11	10	10
Secret Service	1	1	1

*Department of Defense figures represent domestic and overseas positions.
Source: General Accounting Office, April 1980.

Translation Blunders

Interpreters are near the top of the linguists' pecking order. They must translate as they listen. This requires fluency in both languages and also, many linguists say, a special skill that enables the interpreter to put the precise nuance on the translation without consciously pausing to think. When the interpretation goes awry, embarrassment may be the consequence — not only to the interpreter but possibly to the business or national government he represents.

Such was the case on President Carter's trip to Poland in 1977, which was plagued with translation gaffes. His wish to "learn your opinions and understand your desire for the future" came out "I desire the Poles carnally." His interpreter also rendered the president's "when I left my country" as "when I deserted my country."

On a more serious vein was the incorrect translation of remarks made by Soviet leader Nikita S. Khrushchev at a meeting in Moscow in November 1956 held in connection with a Polish-Soviet conference. "We will bury you," Khrushchev was widely quoted at the time as telling the Western leaders attending the meeting. Kremlinologists now agree, however, that what Khrushchev actually said was, "We will be present at your funeral" — a word choice that conveys the notion "we will survive you" rather than "bury you."

Stories of international business blunders also abound. In Taiwan, Pepsi Cola executives failed to realize that their slogan "Come alive with Pepsi" had been translated as "Pepsi brings your ancestors back from the grave." In French-speaking Quebec, faulty advertising of laundry soap can clean out sales, one company discovered. It had described the detergent as suited for the really dirty parts of the wash — *les parties de sale.* Sales plummeted and the company later learned to its chagrin that the phrase meant "private parts."*

*Cited by David A. Ricks, Marilyn Y. C. Fu, Jeffery S. Arpan, *International Business Blunders* (1974), p. 4.

---

school children study Spanish, according to Peter Eddy of the Center for Applied Linguistics.[29] Some are non-Hispanic children living in largely Hispanic communities. As ethnic groups continue to grow in size and importance, the United States will find it increasingly difficult to return to the monolingualism of the turn of the century.

[29] Interview, Aug. 1, 1980.

Selected Bibliography

Books

Andersson, Theodore, and Mildred Boyer, *Bilingual Schooling in the United States*, 2 vols., Southwest Educational Development Laboratory, 1970.

Ricks, David A., Marilyn Y. C. Fu and Jeffrey S. Arpan, *International Business Blunders*, Grid Inc., 1974.

Simon, Paul, *The Tongue-Tied American*, to be published in autumn 1980.

Articles

Eddy, Peter A., "Foreign Language Study in the U.S. Today: Frill or Fundamental?" *Compact*, Vol. XIV, No. 1, spring 1980.

Frith, James R., "Testing the FSI Testing Kit," *Association of Departments of Foreign Languages Bulletin*, Vol. 11, No. 2, November 1979.

Hayden, Samuel L., "Foreign Languages, International Studies, and Business (A Dubious Savior)," *The Annals of the American Academy of Political and Social Science*, May 1980.

Hufstedler, Shirley M., "A World in Transition," *Change*, May-June 1980.

Simon, Paul, "The U.S. Crisis in Foreign Language," *The Annals of the American Academy of Political and Social Science*, May 1980.

Reports and Studies

Center for Applied Linguistics, "Language in Education: Theory and Practice," May 1978.

Editorial Research Reports: "Bilingual Education," 1977 Vol. II, p. 619.

General Accounting Office, "Study of Foreign Languages and Related Areas: Federal Support, Administration, Need," Sept. 13, 1978; "More Competence in Foreign Languages Needed by Federal Personnel Working Overseas," April 15, 1980.

Modern Language Association of America, "Language Study for the 1980s: Reports of the MLA-ACLS Language Task Forces," 1980.

National Education Association, "Foreign Languages — Yesterday, Today and Tomorrow," 1975.

President's Commission on Foreign Language and International Studies, "Strength Through Wisdom, A Critique of U.S. Capability," November 1979.

Rand Corporation, "Foreign Language and International Studies Specialists: The Marketplace and National Policy," September 1979.

University of Idaho, "An Investigation into the Effects of Second Language Learning on Achievement in English," July 1979.

COLLEGE ADMISSIONS

by

John Kotler

**Apr. 11
1 9 8 0**

COLLEGE ADMISSIONS

EVERY year about this time, millions of high school seniors exhibit similar symptoms — bouts of anxiety, irritability and a tendency to wait by the mail box. The object of all these concerns is the letter telling them whether they will be admitted or rejected by the college of their choice. For the most part, the letters arrive by mid-April. The vast majority of college candidates probably have less to worry about than they realize. The number of students in the traditional undergraduate age bracket has declined in recent years *(see p. 111)* and some schools already have fewer applicants than they need to fill their classrooms. As a result, many colleges are aggressively recruiting new students.[1]

Nearly four out of five freshman applicants at public and private four-year colleges now are being accepted, according to a survey published last fall by the American Association of Collegiate Registrars and Admissions Officers (AACRAO) and the College Board, a non-profit education association. Private four-year schools, which usually are thought of as having the toughest entrance requirements, accept more than 77 percent of those who apply. The comparable figures for public two-year colleges and private two-year colleges are 91 percent and 86 percent respectively *(see box, p. 101).*[2]

"The public perception that most colleges accept only a small percentage of persons who apply is simply not true," said James E. Nelson, the College Board's vice president for program research and planning. "The problem may be that the public mostly hears about only a few select, prestigious colleges. In fact, the vast majority of colleges ... are not that hard to get into."

The findings of the College Board-AACRAO survey probably do little to allay the concerns of those who have applied to one of the nation's highly selective universities. Last year Harvard accepted only 2,249 of 13,089 applicants for the freshman class, a rate of 18 percent, followed by 21 percent at Princeton and 24

---

[1] See "College Recruiting," *E.R.R.,* 1974 Vol. II, pp. 661-680.

[2] The results of "The College Board-AACRAO Survey of Undergraduate Admissions Policies, Practices and Procedures" were presented at the College Board's 1979 annual meeting, held Oct. 30 in New Orleans.

percent at Yale.[3] Among the factors that determine who is accepted at the Ivy League and other prestigious schools are scores on college entrance examinations such as the Scholastic Aptitude Test (SAT) prepared for the College Board by the Educational Testing Service. About 1.5 million SATs were administered last year. Nearly a million students took the comparable American College Testing Program (ACT) exam.

Nearly 60 percent of the public four-year colleges and 54 percent of the private four-year schools responding to the College Board-AACRAO survey said that scores on standardized tests were a "very important factor" in admissions decisions. However, more than 27 percent of the public four-year colleges and nearly 40 percent of the private four-year colleges reported that test scores were either "one of several factors" considered or were "a minor factor." About 16 percent of the college officials surveyed said that SAT and ACT scores were less important today in making admissions decisions than in 1970. Although 40 percent of the institutions reported having a minimum grade point average below which applicants generally were not considered eligible for admission, less than 30 percent indicated having similar "minimum standards" for SAT scores.

Debate Over Use of Entrance Examinations

Using test scores as admissions criteria can present problems, as major testing organizations readily admit. The College Board issued guidelines in 1977 warning that test scores are "approximate rather than exact" measures of academic potential. "Test scores, like all types of measurements, physical as well as psychological, are not perfectly precise and should not be treated as though they were," the guidelines stated. The following year the board issued another warning to college admissions officers. "Test scores should not be the sole factor in determining the admission of an applicant . . . ," the board cautioned. "In most instances a student's high school record is the best available predictor of academic success in college, and a combination of high school record and scores is almost always better than either one alone."[4]

Despite such warnings some people believe college entrance examinations still play too large a role in college admissions. Consumer activist Ralph Nader recently issued a report that was highly critical of standardized entrance examinations, especially the SAT and other tests provided by the Educational Testing Service. In the preface to the report, Nader called the SAT a "one-time, three-hour gamble which can determine a

---

[3] Figures reported by Gene I. Maeroff in *The New York Times,* April 4, 1980.
[4] The College Board, "Taking the SAT," 1978, p. 48.

Freshmen Applicants Accepted and Enrolled By Type of College

	Public Two-Year	Public Four-Year	Private Four-Year	Private Two-Year
Freshmen Applicants Accepted for Admission	90.7%	78.6%	77.5%	86.2%
Freshmen Applicants Actually Enrolled	77.3	53.2	47.7	65.5
Accepted Freshmen Applicants Actually Enrolled	81.3	65.8	59.8	73.5

Source: The College Board and the American Association of Collegiate Registrars and Admissions Officers, 1979.

life's pathway."[5] The report said the SAT and other ETS examinations, such as the Law School Admissions Test (LSAT), are used to limit access to the most selective undergraduate and professional schools and, thus, to the upper strata of American society. It cited studies which indicate that test scores often break down along socio-economic lines with the children of wealthy, educated parents consistently receiving high scores, while children of poor families generally score lowest. One reason for this, the report stated, is that the SAT has built-in cultural biases that make it difficult for minority members to score as well as their white counterparts.

The College Board contends that the SAT and other standardized tests have helped minorities, not harmed them. George H. Hanford, president of the College Board, believes standardized tests have allowed colleges to identify talented minority students who might otherwise have been overlooked. Edward A. Wynne, editor of *Character,* a magazine that focuses on public and private policies which affect young people, made a similar point. "Before the tests, [admissions] decisions were more individualized, and [colleges] used more and softer information," he wrote recently. "As a result, the decision makers were more prone to apply time-saving criteria such as the reputation of the applicant's high school, or whether he had relatives as alumni."[6]

In a memo to College Board members in February, Hanford acknowledged that minority students generally score below other students on the SAT. But he said this reflects their poor educational backgrounds not a bias on the exam. "The test does not create the difference, it mirrors and reveals it," he wrote.

---

[5] Allan Nairn and Associates, "The Reign of ETS: The Ralph Nader Report on the Educational Testing Service," January 1980, pp. xii-xiii.

[6] Writing in *The Wall Street Journal,* Feb. 14, 1980.

Hanford also claimed minority students have had more success entering college during the past decade than many people realize. From 1970 to 1977, he said, college enrollment increased 5 percent for blacks and 6 percent for Hispanics while it remained fairly constant for white students.

Perhaps the most serious charge in the Nader report was that the SAT is not very useful in predicting college success. Pure chance, "a role of the dice," would tell as much about a student's chances for success in the first year of college in 88 percent of the cases, the report said. Hanford sharply disagreed. In his February memo he cited the results of a 13-year study of the 19 colleges in the Georgia state university system that indicated that SAT scores provide "a strong, incremental addition" to the validity of admissions predictions when used in conjunction with high school grades.[7]

Even if the tests are helpful in predicting academic achievement, it is generally conceded that they tell little about success in later life. Attributes like drive, ingenuity and interpersonal skills seem to play a greater role in long-term achievement than either grades or test scores. Nader, in his preface to the report on the ETS, called for "broader, more diverse approaches for assessing individual performance . . . a multi-cultural array of evaluations, which can tap the untapped or unique talents of diverse individuals."

Some colleges use entrance examinations as a tool to assess student weaknesses rather than as a selective device. This seems to be especially true of the ACT exam, which is used by many colleges in the South, West and Midwest. Bob Elliot of ACT's Iowa City office said the test is designed primarily to aid high school and college counselors help students choose career and study paths, although it is also used for predicting academic performance.[8] Some educators believe all college entrance exams will be utilized less for selecting students and more for guiding them in the coming years.

Recent Enactment of 'Truth-in-Testing' Laws

Criticism of standardized entrance examinations has resulted in passage of "truth-in-testing" laws in California and New York. A national truth-in-testing law is being considered in Congress, and similar measures are being pushed in a number of states. The law passed by the California legislature in 1978 re-

---

[7] The Georgia study found that the SAT alone provided a correlation of 0.49 (out of a perfect 1.0) with success in the freshman year, compared to a 0.54 correlation for high school grades. Used together, however, the two measures provided a correlation of 0.65.

[8] Interview, April 3, 1980.

quires testing companies to provide the public with sample tests similar to the actual exams administered in the state. In July 1979, the New York legislature approved a more stringent law. It requires companies to provide the questions and answers for actual tests to those who request them after the scores are released.[9] The law was backed by the Parent-Teacher Association (PTA), the National Education Association and the American Federation of Teachers (AFL-CIO).

The truth-in-testing bill introduced in Congress in July 1979 is now before the House Education and Labor Committee. The bill has a disclosure requirement similar to the New York law. In addition, it would require the makers of standardized tests to provide test takers with a "clear overview" of the examination prior to administering the tests and to publicize the results of studies concerning the validity and reliability of entrance examinations. Supporters have said they are reviewing the bill and may submit a somewhat different version in the next few months.

At a press conference on April 7, President George H. Hanford announced that the College Board was taking a number of steps to give students more information about the content of tests and provide them with procedures for challenging test scores. Every autumn the board will publish one version of the exam that was used during the preceding year, along with a statistical analysis of its characteristics. Students taking the SAT will have an opportunity to verify their scores personally by receiving their answer sheet, a scoring key and scoring information. The fee for this optional service will be refunded if any discrepancy is found.

Hanford coupled his announcement with criticism of truth-in-testing laws, which he said "imposed misguided operational requirements which threaten test quality." The board has asked Congress and the state legislatures not to enact any new disclosure laws until there has been time to evaluate the effects of the New York law.

Diane Ravitch of Columbia University's Teachers College, believes the New York law will "accomplish few, if any, of its intended purposes." Instead of making tests less culturally biased, she said, the law will make it more difficult and expensive for test companies to take the time they now do to screen out questions which are slanted against minorities. She also said the law will have little effect on admissions procedures since most college admissions officers already understand the weaknesses of

---

[9] The New York law went into effect Jan. 1, 1980. The first SAT covered by the law was administered March 22. The courts have granted medical schools in the state a delay in implementing the law for their entrance exams.

tests and treat them accordingly. Some highly selective colleges will establish their own entrance exams if they feel disclosure is making standardized tests less reliable, she concluded.[10]

Some educators worry that disclosure of test answers will help so-called "coaching" schools, which specialize in preparing students to take college entrance and other standardized tests. On the other hand, the effectiveness of these schools has been questioned. The College Board and the Educational Testing Service maintain that coaching or "cramming" does little good because the tests measure general aptitude and skills developed over years of learning. However, a study of two coaching schools in the Boston area published last year by the Federal Trade Commission indicated that coaching might help certain underachievers who do well in school but who do not perform well on standardized tests.[11]

Continued Concern Over Drop in Test Scores

SAT scores have been declining for nearly two decades, although the drop has leveled off somewhat in the last few years *(see box, p. 105)*. The average score on the verbal sectin of the test declined from 478 in 1962-63 to 426 in 1978-79. The average score on the math section dropped from 502 in 1962-63 to 466 in 1978-79. The tests are scored on a scale from 200 to 800. From 1972 to 1979 the proportion of college-bound students scoring in the 600 to 800 range declined to 7 percent from 11 percent on the verbal section and to 15 percent from 17 percent on the math section.

Scores on tests administered by the American College Testing Program also have fallen in recent years. The average composite score of the ACT tests, which are taken by some 900,000 high school students annually in English, math, social studies and natural sciences, declined from 19.9 in 1969-70 to 18.6 in 1978-79. The ACT scale ranges from 1 to 36.

Concerned about the trend, the College Entrance Examination Board set up an advisory panel headed by former Secretary of Labor Willard Wirtz in 1975 to look into the test-score decline. The panel's report, issued in August 1977, found no single force or closely related set of forces responsible for the decline. The panel concluded that there were two stages in the decline — one between 1963 and 1970, and the other after 1970. The first decline was caused by "compositional" changes in the student population taking the tests, the Wirtz panel said. Each year between 1963 and 1970, those taking the tests "included larger

---

[10] Writing in *The New York Times*, Aug. 15, 1979.

[11] "Effects of Coaching on Standardized Examinations," Federal Trade Commission, Bureau of Consumer Protection, March 1979.

National Test Scores

| School Year | SAT[1] Score Averages | | ACT[2] Score Averages |
	Verbal	Mathematical	Composite
1962-63	478	502	NA[3]
1963-64	475	498	NA[3]
1964-65	473	498	19.9
1965-66	471	496	20.0
1966-67	467	495	19.4
1967-68	466	494	19.0
1968-69	462	491	19.4
1969-70	460	488	19.9
1970-71	454	487	19.2
1971-72	450	482	19.1
1972-73	443	481	19.2
1973-74	440	478	18.9
1974-75	437	473	18.6
1975-76	429	470	18.3
1976-77	429	471	18.4
1977-78	429	469	18.5
1978-79	426	466	18.6

[1] Scholastic Aptitude Test. Scale ranges from 200 to 800.
[2] American College Testing Program. Scale ranges from 1 to 36.
[3] Not Available.

Source: College Entrance Examination Board and the American College Testing Program.

proportions of characteristically lower-scoring groups of students" — who were identified mainly as children of poor or black families and girls, who average lower scores on the math section. "This pulled the overall average down."[12]

The post-1970 decline, the panel reported, probably was caused by many factors, including: (1) the movement away from basics and to elective courses, especially in English, (2) "clearly observable evidence of diminished seriousness of purpose and attention to mastery of skills and knowledge in the learning process as it proceeds in the schools, the home, and the society generally," (3) higher divorce rates, (4) the prevalence of television watching and (5) an "apparent diminution in young people's learning motivation."

U.S. colleges have adjusted to the declining test scores by lowering their own admissions requirements. Approximately 43 percent of the schools responding to the College Board-AACRAO survey said that they expected higher admissions test scores from applicants in 1970 than they did in 1978. Declining scores on college entrance examinations have been interpreted

---

[12] College Entrance Examination Board, "On Further Examination: Report of the Advisory Panel on the Scholastic Aptitude Test Score Decline," 1977, p. 13.

by many to mean that the quality of American education is slipping. A study conducted by the National Association of Secondary School Principals found that students scored considerably higher SAT scores at schools that stressed academic courses such as mathematics, foreign languages, English and physical science than students at schools that experimented with new approaches in curriculum content. The schools across the country where SAT scores rose, the study found, "took certain initiatives or else maintained some specific 'standards' that they considered important to the success of their college-bound students."[13]

Changing Admissions Criteria

U NTIL the late 19th century, most American colleges maintained their own special entrance requirements and prescribed their own courses of study for prospective students. Many established preparatory academies to help youngsters get ready for college studies. If the college did not have its own academy, college-bound students enrolled in another academy or worked with a private tutor who "fitted" them for the college's requirements. Entrance examinations consisted of the college president and several faculty members questioning the candidate on his studies in Latin, Greek and mathematics — the essential ingredients of a classical education. The examinations often went from dawn to dusk, with only a short break for lunch. According to education historian Harold S. Wechsler, "the decision to admit a student . . . was determined by the quality of his answers, the college's financial picture, and not infrequently on the kindliness of a faculty member."[14] As subjects such as geography, English grammar, algebra and history were added to the entrance requirements, many colleges replaced the oral examinations with a battery of written tests.

Colleges sought to strengthen their position in American society by portraying themselves as "capstones" of a system "from which the next generation of American leaders would emerge." To succeed, they needed cooperation from the private academies and later the public high schools in tailoring secondary school curriculum to fit college requirements. But the diversity of college entrance requirements made the task difficult. Wilson Farrand, headmaster of Newark Academy, explained the problem in a speech he gave in 1895: "Princeton and Columbia call

---

[13] National Association of Secondary School Principals, "Guidelines for Improving SAT Scores," 1978, p. 4.

[14] Harold S. Wechsler, *The Qualified Student* (1977), p. 7.

for six books of the *Aeneid;* Yale requires, in addition, the *Ecologues*. These do not count for maximum standing at Princeton unless combined with the *Georgics* ... Princeton requires Latin of candidates for one course, but not for the others. Yale demands it of all, Columbia of none."[15]

While colleges and high schools in the East continued to bicker over entrance requirements, the University of Michigan pioneered a new system of accepting all graduates of high schools that had been accredited by a team of faculty inspectors. The plan was championed by Harry S. Frieze, a professor who served as acting president of the university in 1870-71. Frieze modeled the Michigan plan on the German gymnasia, secondary schools which prepared students for the university. Many of those who supported admission by certificate, Wechsler wrote, saw it as a "potential solution for solving a basic problem faced by most American colleges in the 19th century — the need to maintain and if possible to increase enrollments."[16] Only 5 percent of American 17-year-olds graduated from high school in 1890, and only a fraction of this group went on to college. Many colleges adopted the certificate system with the expectation that more students would seek admission once demanding entrance examinations were dropped. As more institutions joined the movement, regional associations were established to assume responsibility for inspecting and accrediting secondary schools.

By the turn of the century, the certificate system had become the most popular method of regulating college admissions. It gained strongest acceptance in the Midwest, where the movement began. Resistance was strongest in the older, elite colleges of New England and the Middle Atlantic States. "Such institutions," Wechsler wrote, "opposed certification because it was new and they revered traditions; because it threatened their domination of the high schools...; and because it implied that they were in competition for students, something their high enrollments did not support in fact and their high self-estimate did not allow in principle."[17] In time, however, all of the Ivy League schools except Harvard, Princeton and Yale joined the system.

Estabishment of the College Board in 1900

The elite colleges were never comfortable with the certificate system, but neither were they satisfied with widely divergent

---

[15] From Farrand's inaugural address as president of the Schoolmaster's Association of New York and vicinity, Oct. 12, 1895. His topic was "The Reform of College Entrance Requirements."

[16] Wechsler, *op. cit.*, p. 20.

[17] *Ibid.*, p. 57.

standards for college entrance. Presidents Nicholas Murray But-
ler of Columbia and Charles W. Eliot of Harvard led the campaign to bring about closer cooperation between institutions of
higher learning and secondary schools, while keeping the final
decision on admissions with the colleges. Their efforts cul-
minated in the creation of the College Entrance Examination
Board in 1900.[18]

The College Board, as it came to be known, supplied standardized entrance examinations to its members. Only 12 schools
were members at the beginning: Barnard, Bryn Mawr, Columbia, Cornell, Johns Hopkins, New York University, University of
Pennsylvania, Rutgers, Swarthmore, Union, Vassar and Wom-
en's College of Baltimore. Gradually the board attracted more
members, who saw in it the chance to reach a larger and more
varied group of students. Examinations soon were available to
students throughout the nation. By 1910, even "The Big Three"
— Harvard, Yale and Princeton — had joined the fold.

The original College Board tests were essay examinations that
measured a student's retention of specific facts. But educators
soon began to question whether such tests identified candidates
who would succeed in college. Following World War I, the College Board became interested in testing programs developed by
the government to measure soldiers' aptitude for various assignments. In 1926 the board administered its first aptitude test, the
SAT, a multiple choice exam covering a wide variety of topics.
The goal of the aptitude test was to measure "future ability"
rather than "past mastery." The tests were supposed to "reveal
the broad expanse of a student's knowledge, not the minute details of his preparation."[19] The board continued to offer the
older essay examinations, but most colleges preferred the new
SAT. Most of the older exams were dropped during World War
II and never resumed.

By 1946, the College Board had expanded its testing program
far beyond college entrance examinations. Among its clients
were the U.S. Department of State, the Bureau of Naval Personnel, the U.S. Naval Academy, the Coast Guard Academy and
the National Administrative Board for the Pepsi-Cola Scholarships. Many members felt the board had strayed too far from its
original mandate to provide college entrance examinations. On
Dec. 19, 1947, the board, in cooperation with the Carnegie
Foundation for the Advancement of Teaching and the American
Council on Education, established the Educational Testing Service (ETS). The new organization was to assume responsibility

---

[18] See Claude M. Fuess, *The College Board, Its First Fifty Years* (1967).

[19] Wechsler, *op. cit.*, pp. 247-248.

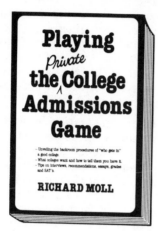
for developing all the tests formerly handled by the board itself. The board would focus its attention entirely on the tests used by high schools and colleges. It would have broad policy authority over the content of the exams and also handle such matters as the location and frequency of various tests.

Efforts to Expand U.S. College Population

A report published by the President's Commission on Higher Education in 1946 noted that only a fraction of those who could benefit from higher education actually were enrolled in colleges. "American colleges must envision a much larger role for higher education in the national life," the commission stated. "They can no longer consider themselves merely the instrument for producing an intellectual elite; they must become the means by which every citizen, youth and adult, is enabled and encouraged to carry his education, formal and informal, as far as his native capacities permit."

For 20 years following the end of World War II American colleges and universities experienced unparalleled growth and expansion. The beginning of this new era in higher education came with the passage of the Servicemen's Readjustment Act of 1944 — the G.I. Bill — "the largest scholarship program in the nation's history." The federal government provided veterans who were enrolled as full-time students with living allowances and made direct payments to the institution for tuition, fees, and laboratory, library and other normal school costs.

The coming of age of the "baby boom" generation born after World War II shot college enrollment up in the 1960s. Between 1959-60 and 1969-70 enrollment more than doubled, rising from 3,471,000 to some 7,978,000. Not only was there a large increase in the number of persons of college age, but the proportion going to college also rose. By 1970, 34 percent of the 18-21 age group were enrolled in degree-credit programs in higher education, compared with 23 percent in 1960, 15 percent in 1950 and 11 percent in 1940.

The social pressures to go to college increased enormously during the 1960s. Higher education not only was seen as the most likely path to economic success and individual fulfillment, but a steady rise in per capita income throughout the decade meant that more parents could afford to send their children to college than ever before. And as more and more persons obtained degrees, employers began recruiting college graduates for jobs that had formerly gone to persons with a high school education.

At the same time that a college degree became an essential component of the American Dream, it became more difficult to obtain. As enrollments soared in the late 1950s and the 1960s, many private institutions, and some public ones, began to limit enrollment and raise admission standards. Increased emphasis was placed on a student's performance on national college aptitude tests, including the Scholastic Aptitude Test (SAT) administered by the College Board. So great was the demand for student ability screening that another national testing service, the American College Testing Program (ACT), was founded in 1959 in Iowa City, Iowa.

One of the most dynamic developments in higher education during this period was the growth of two-year community colleges. Vocationally oriented junior colleges had been around since the mid-19th century, but they remained a minor facet of American education until the late 1950s. By the mid-1960s these colleges, by now being called community colleges, were opening at a rate of about one a week. In the 1959-60 school year, some 640,500 students were enrolled in two-year colleges. A decade later, the number had grown to almost two million full- and part-time students, nearly 30 percent of all undergraduates in the nation. The rapid advance of community colleges was attributed to their open-admissions policies, their geographic distribution across the country, and their usually low tuition fees.

Future Enrollment Patterns

F OR MUCH of its history, the story of American higher education was one of growth and expansion. But times have changed. After more than a quarter-century of uninterrupted growth, college enrollments started levelling off in the mid-1970s. The number of people enrolled in the nation's colleges and universities is expected to decline in the 1980s *(see graph, p. 113)*. This view is supported by Census Bureau projections that the country's college-age population will shrink 18 percent between 1980 and 1990, with most of the drop — 11 percent — occurring during the first half of the decade. By 1985, there will be 1.7 million fewer 18-to-21-year olds than in 1980.

The projected enrollment drop threatens many institutions with both financial and educational problems. From an economic standpoint, colleges may be faced with declining tuition payments at a time of steadily increasing costs. Many small private colleges could go out of business.[20] Public colleges and universities probably will face the loss of some programs as a result of federal and state budget cuts. Even the most financially stable institutions may have to reduce their programs and faculties if the number of students declines significantly.

Faced with the prospects of waning enrollment for the remainder of the decade, colleges and universities have begun to broaden their recruiting efforts. Many are aiming their pitch at adults. Students 25 and older numbered 1.7 million and accounted for 22 percent of the campus population in 1970. By 1975 these figures had jumped to 34 percent and 3.7 million and, according to a Census Bureau estimate, four of every 10 collegians may be above 25 by 1985 if current enrollment rates by age continue at the prevailing pace.

A report published recently by the Carnegie Council on Policy Studies in Higher Education said that projected increases in the number of older students during the next two decades will offset about 9 percent of the projected drop in the number of students aged 18-25. "Participation rates for adults with prior college attendance may rise to even higher levels than past practice might indicate . . . ," the report concluded, "because of the great

---

[20] See "Future of Private Colleges," *E.R.R.*, 1976 Vol. I, pp. 305-322.

competition of many to get ahead within the bulge of young adults, because of the desire of some to change jobs in the face of this competition, and because of the impulse of a few to escape the competition by attention to non-vocational interests."[21]

Robert Hawkes Jr., dean of the division of continuing education at George Mason University in Fairfax City, Va., calls the burgeoning of adult education "the quiet revolution," as opposed to the "turbulent" era of college demonstrations in the 1960s. He believes the latest revolution "will have an even larger impact" than the earlier one. "For the most part," he said recently, adults "are incredibly good students," something U.S. educators first learned when veterans began enrolling in colleges after World War II with the aid of the G.I. Bill.[22]

The Wall Street Journal recently reported that 500,000 executives take advanced management courses every year, ranging from weekend seminars to degree-granting programs lasting a year or more. Many colleges send their professors off campus to teach executives on their home ground. Some educators have strong reservations about the off-campus programs, however. Often they provide "little more than poor quality education delivered anywhere to any student for monetary gain," said Kay Anderson, director of an accrediting agency for schools in California and Hawaii.[23]

Increase in Foreign Student Enrollments

The crisis in Iran and President Carter's subsequent order to deport some Iranian students has heightened the nation's awareness of foreign students in American universities. Their numbers have increased fivefold over the last two decades, from 50,000 in 1960 to more than 260,000 today. In the past, colleges admitted foreign students primarily to add to the diversity of campus life. Today the motive often is money. Richard Farmer, chairman of the department of international business at Indiana University in Bloomington, has calculated that the average foreign student spends $10,000 a year for tuition, fees, books, travel and other costs.[24]

Students from oil exporting countries have come to the United States in increasing numbers in recent years. Those from nations in the Organization of Petroleum Exporting Countries

---

[21] "Three Thousand Futures: The Next 20 Years for Higher Education," Final Report of the Carnegie Council on Policy Studies in Higher Education, 1980, p. 37.

[22] Quoted by James T. Yenckel in *The Washington Post*, March 17, 1980.

[23] Quoted by Andy Pasztor and Rich Jaroslovsky in *The Wall Street Journal*, May 21, 1979.

[24] Quoted by Edward B. Fiske in a series of stories on recruitment of foreign students appearing in *The New York Times*, Feb. 24-25, 1980.

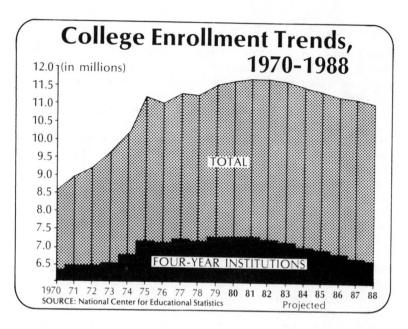

College Enrollment Trends, 1970-1988

12.0 (in millions)

TOTAL

FOUR-YEAR INSTITUTIONS

1970 71 72 73 74 75 76 77 78 79 80 81 82 83 84 85 86 87 88

SOURCE: National Center for Educational Statistics

Projected

(OPEC) make up about a third of all foreign students compared to only 12 percent in 1971-72. Iran leads the list of foreign nations sending students to the United States, with at least 45,000 studying in this country. Nigeria is second with 16,200. Saudi Arabia, Venezuela and Mexico each send more than 5,000. Many foreign students in the United States come from South and East Asia. Taiwan now has about 15,400 students here, Hong Kong and Japan more than 10,000, and Thailand more than 5,000. China, which is just beginning to sample the U.S. college market, has sent about 1,000 students so far, including the son of Deng Xiaoping, the senior Deputy Prime Minister.

Graduate students make up about 44 percent of the foreign college students. The National Academy of Science reported in 1977 that foreign students received 42 percent of the doctoral degrees awarded by American institutions in engineering and 25 percent of those in physics and mathematics. There is some concern that foreign students are taking college seats away from Americans; but it is pointed out that there is a shortage of U.S. applicants for many graduate programs which attract foreign students such as civil engineering. In the elite schools, entrance requirements usually are much stricter for foreigners than for U.S. students.

Problems Created by Rising Tuition Costs

Getting into college may be easier in the 1980s, but paying for it is likely to become more difficult. College costs rose nearly 70 percent in the last decade, and inflation is expected to push them higher in the years ahead. Tuition increases announced at many public and private colleges for the 1980-81 school year match or even exceed last year's 13 percent inflation rate. Students enrolling at the Massachusetts Institute of Technology next fall will pay $6,200 tuition for the year, 17 percent higher than the previous year. Stanford University has announced a 12.3 percent increase to $6,285 a year, Harvard a 13.2 percent increase to $6,000, the University of Chicago a 13.3 percent increase to $5,100 and Clark University a 16.1 percent increase to $5,400.[25]

Proposals to increase federal aid to college students are in jeopardy as the president and Congress seek to balance the 1981 federal budget. Administration officials have branded as "inflationary" a bill that would raise Basic Educational Opportunity Grants (BEOGs) by $2.1 billion in fiscal 1981 and increase the total cost of federal student aid to $11 billion by 1985. The bill, which was approved by the House in 1979, would allow increases in both the maximum cash awards to individual students, to $2,520 from $1,800, and the percentage of college costs that the grants could cover — to 70 percent from 50 percent in existing law. A similar bill now is before the Senate Labor and Human Resources Education Subcommittee.[26]

Congress has been debating new approaches to federal student aid. Legislation to provide federal tuition tax credits to parents gathered broad support in both houses of Congress in 1978, but the measure died after President Carter said he would veto it. The administration opposed the measure on the ground that it would benefit all families regardless of economic need rather than concentrating resources on low-income families.[27]

Some educators believe the primary burden of paying for a college education should fall on the student, not his or her family. John Silber, president of Boston University, has proposed a plan to provide tuition advances of up to $5,000 a year, up to a total of $15,000, for students who successfully complete their freshman year of college. After graduation the student would begin paying back the tuition advance at the rate of 2 percent of his gross annual income. There would be no interest, per se, but the student would owe a 50 percent surcharge which would go into an endowment fund to support the program. A person who borrowed the maximum amount of $15,000 would have to pay an additional $7,500. Silber justified the extra fee by pointing to Census Bureau figures which show that the average male college

---

[25] Reported by Jack Magarrell in "Many Colleges Plan 2-Digit Increases in Tuition to Keep Up With Inflation," *The Chronicle of Higher Education,* March 3, 1980.

[26] See Congressional Quarterly *Weekly Report,* March 1, 1980, p. 630.

[27] See "College Tuition Costs," *E.R.R.,* 1978 Vol. I, pp. 141-160 and *1978 CQ Almanac,* p. 248.

graduate earns about $232,000 more during a lifetime than a male high school graduate. Critics of the proposal contend that such a large debt — $22,500 to cover the maximum advance and surcharge — is too great a burden for most graduates to carry.

Opportunities in New Admissions Climate

The coming decade may fulfill the mandate of the 1946 President's Commission on Higher Education which envisioned a system of higher education in which every citizen could participate. Demographic trends may do more for the cause of universal college education than the best laid plans of educators or government officials. The Carnegie Council predicts that during the next 20 years students "will be recruited more actively, admitted more readily, retained more assiduously, counseled more attentively, graded more considerately, financed more adequately, taught more conscientiously, placed in jobs more insistently, and the curriculum will be more tailored to their tastes."[28]

Some educators wonder what the trend toward mass college education will mean for academic standards. There already are complaints that today's students are unprepared for college-level studies and that many lack even basic skills in English and mathematics. Theodore L. Gross, former dean of humanities at the City College of New York during that institution's experiment with "open admissions" and now provost of the Capital Campus of Pennsylvania State University, has called for a National Center for Literacy which would explore ways to ensure that high school students are well grounded in English and writing skills before they reach college.[29]

Many educators feel that the challenge of mass higher education can become an opportunity for colleges and other institutions of higher learning to expand their own horizons, a chance to rethink the American educational system. Colleges have adapted to the needs of new groups of students in the past, and they can do so again, it is argued. As the competition for college entrance subsides, admissions officers and professors may be able to spend more time and effort on developing programs to meet the diverse needs of the student population. Admissions tests might be used to learn more about applicants rather than as a tool to select or reject them. The 1980s, it seems, is a crossroad for higher education. The choices that are made will determine the fate of a generation of students and of the colleges themselves.

---

[28] "Three Thousand Futures," *op. cit.*, p. 54.

[29] Theodore L. Gross, *Academic Turmoil* (1980), pp. 166-221.

Selected Bibliography

Books

Barton, David W. Jr., Ed., *Marketing of Higher Education,* Jossey-Bass Inc., 1978.

Fuess, Claude M., *The College Board: The First Fifty Years,* College Entrance Examination Board, 1967.

Gross, Theodore L., *Academic Turmoil,* Anchor Press-Doubleday, 1980.

Marland, Sidney P. Jr., *The College Board and the Twentieth Century,* College Entrance Examination Board, 1975.

Moll, Richard, *Playing the Private College Admissions Game,* Times Books, 1979.

Sacks, Herbert S., et. al., *Hurdles: The Admissions Dilemma in American Higher Education,* Atheneum, 1978.

Wechsler, Harold S., *The Qualified Student,* John Wiley & Sons, Inc., 1977.

Articles

Chase, Alston, "Financing A College Education," *Atlantic,* April 1980.

"Controversy In Congress Over Federal Student-Aid Policy," *Congressional Digest,* January 1979.

Fallows, James, "The Tests and the 'Brightest': How Fair Are The College Boards?" *Atlantic,* February 1980.

Farnsworth, Kent A., "Selling the Student Consumer," *Change,* November-December 1979.

Fiske, Edward B., "The Marketing of the Colleges," *Atlantic,* October 1979.

Jencks, Christopher, "Why Students Aren't Learning," *The Center Magazine,* July-August 1979.

Nader, Ralph, "Student Power 101," *Change,* November-December 1979.

Sewall, Gil, et. al., "Tests: How Good? How Fair?," *Time,* Feb. 18, 1980.

Smith, R. Jeffrey, " 'Truth-in-Testing' Attracts Diverse Support," *Science,* September 1979.

Reports and Studies

Carnegie Council on Policy Studies in Higher Education:"Opportunity For Women in Higher Education," 1973; "Selective Admissions in Higher Education," 1977; "Three Thousand Futures: The Next 20 Years For Higher Education," Final Report, 1980.

College Board-American Association of College Registrars and Admissions Officers, "Survey of Admissions Policies, Practices and Procedures," Sept. 20, 1979.

College Board, "On Further Examination: Report of the Advisory Panel on the Scholastic Aptitude Test Score Decline," 1977.

Editorial Research Reports: "College Recruiting," 1974 Vol. II, p. 61; "Future of Private Colleges," 1976 Vol. I, p. 305; "College Tuition Costs," 1978 Vol I, p. 141; "Competency Tests," 1978 Vol. II, p. 601.

Federal Trade Commission, Bureau of Consumer Protection, "Effects of Coaching on Standardized Admission Examinations," Revised Statistical Analysis, March 1979.

Nairn, Allan and Associates, "The Reign of ETS-The Ralph Nader Report on the Educational Testing Service," January 1980.

Educating Gifted Children

by

Sandra Stencel

Sept. 14
1 9 7 9

EDUCATING GIFTED CHILDREN

EARLIER this year a married couple in McHenry, Ill., sued their local school district for $1 million. They claimed the school district had failed to provide their 10-year-old son with an education equal to his abilities. First labeled a behavior problem and then said to have a learning disability, the boy was found to have an IQ of 169.[1] Because of his undisciplined behavior, he at first was denied admission to a 12-week program for gifted children — a program his father described as "mostly arts and crafts with a few field trips run by a volunteer." After the boy was given permission to enroll in a high school Spanish class, the permission was revoked when the local school board expressed concern about establishing a precedent. The principal of his elementary school described him as "the kind of child a teacher dreams of having once in a lifetime." "But," he added, "now that we have him we don't know what to do with him."[2]

The Illinois case points up the plight of America's gifted and talented youth. Special programs for the gifted have mushroomed in recent years. State and federal funding for such programs has increased significantly. But according to a recent survey, "the United States still falls far short of meeting the educational needs of this special segment of its population."[3] Dr. Dorothy A. Sisk, director of the U.S. Office of Education's Office of Gifted and Talented, estimates that only 12 percent of the nation's exceptionally bright children and youth are receiving all the educational services they require.[4] John Grossi, director of gifted and talented policy for the Council for Exceptional Children in Reston, Va., said recently that only 41 percent of gifted and talented youth are receiving any special educational services.[5]

---

[1] IQ or intelligence quotient is a number used to express the apparent relative intelligence of a person determined by dividing his mental age as reported on a standardized test by his chronological age and multiplying by 100. An IQ of 130 or higher generally is considered in the gifted range. See Berkley Rice, "Brave New World of Intelligence Testing," *Psychology Today*, September 1979, pp. 26-41.
[2] Quoted in *Time*, April 23, 1979, p. 85.
[3] Patricia Mitchell and Donald Erickson, "The Education of Gifted and Talented Children: A Status Report," *Exceptional Children*, September 1978, p. 13.
[4] Dorothy A. Sisk, "What is Leadership Training for the Gifted?" paper presented at the Third Annual Northern Virginia Conference on Gifted/Talented Education, Manassas, Va., March 3-4, 1978.
[5] Remarks made on "The MacNeil/Lehrer Report," Public Broadcasting Service, April 20, 1979. The Council for Exceptional Children, founded in 1922, works to advance the education of exceptional children and youth, both handicapped and gifted.

Ambivalent attitudes in this country toward those with un-common talents contribute to confused and often contradictory public policy concerning education of gifted students. Most educators now acknowledge that the social, emotional and edu-cational problems of the exceptionally bright can be just as complicated as those of the physically and mentally handi-capped. Yet the problems of the gifted do not easily arouse the public's sympathies. There is a widespread belief that gifted children, because of their extraordinary abilities, ought to be able to make it on their own, and that limited educational resources are better spent on those who cannot.

"In American society there is a love-hate relationship with giftedness and talent," James J. Gallagher and Patricia Weiss wrote in a recent report published by the Council for Basic Education, a non-profit educational association in Washington, D.C. "On the one hand, we revere the gifted individual who has risen from humble background. We are proud to live in a society where talent can triumph over poor environment or limited family status. On the other, our nation began by battling an aristocratic elite and we are strong in our commitment to egali-tarianism. We do not wish a new elite class to develop. As a result, we waver in our attitudes. We design our elementary and secondary school programs for gifted students in ways that can be defended by careful administrators as giving no special fa-vors, no tipping the scales in favor of the powerful or specially endowed."[6]

Defining Who Are the Gifted and Talented

No one knows precisely how many gifted and talented chil-dren there are in the United States. Educators generally agree that between 3 and 5 percent of the school-age population falls into this category. The Council for Exceptional Children es-timates that there are at least 1.3 million gifted students in American schools today. One problem in determining the exact number is the divergence of opinion about what actually con-stitutes giftedness. Up to the end of the 1950s the definition of giftedness was pretty straightforward. It included those children who performed in an advanced fashion on measures of verbal development and logical thinking as measured by standard IQ tests.

The definition of giftedness was broadened in the 1960s when it became apparent that the native ability of minority and disadvantaged youths was not always detected by standardized

---

[6] James J. Gallagher and Patricia Weiss, "The Education of Gifted and Talented Stu-dents: A History and Prospectus," Council for Basic Education, 1979, pp. 1-2. Gallagher is director of the Frank Porter Graham Child Development Center and professor of education at the University of North Carolina. Weiss is an instructor at the University of North Carolina.

Gifted and Talented Children, 1976-77 School Year

State	School Population	G/T School Population*	Receiving Services	% Receiving Services
Ala.	752,507	22,575	N.A.**	—
Alaska	91,190	2,736	N.A.	—
Ariz.	502,817	15,085	9,000	59.7
Ark.	460,593	13,818	N.A.	—
Calif.	4,380,300	131,409	198,000	150.7
Colo.	570,000	17,100	322	1.9
Conn.	635,000	19,050	7,100	37.3
Del.	122,273	3,668	1,300	35.4
Fla.	1,537,336	46,120	N.A.	—
Ga.	1,095,142	32,854	24,340	74.1
Hawaii	174,943	5,248	N.A.	—
Idaho	200,005	6,000	1,200	20.0
Ill.	2,238,129	67,144	N.A.	—
Ind.	1,163,179	34,895	N.A.	—
Iowa	605,127	18,154	N.A.	—
Kan.	436,526	13,096	1,500	11.5
Ky.	694,000	20,820	N.A.	—
La.	839,499	25,185	2,000	7.9
Maine	248,822	7,465	N.A.	—
Md.	860,922	25,828	20,000	77.4
Mass.	1,168,837(est.)	35,065(est.)	N.A.	—
Mich.	2,035,703	61,071	1,600	2.6
Minn.	862,591	25,878	24,000	92.7
Miss.	510,209	15,306	2,100	13.7
Mo.	950,142	28,504	4,263	15.0
Mont.	170,552	5,117	500	9.8
Neb.	312,024	9,361	8,540	91.2
Nev.	141,791	4,254	N.A.	—
N.H.	175,496	5,265	N.A.	—
N.J.	1,427,000	42,810	5,700	13.3
N.M.	284,719	8,542	911	10.7
N.Y.	3,378,997	101,370	N.A.	—
N.C.	1,191,316	35,739	39,691	111.1
N.D.	129,106	3,873	188	4.9
Ohio	2,249,440	67,483	14,000	20.7
Okla.	597,665	17,930	2,006	11.2
Ore.	474,707	14,241	N.A.	—
Pa.	2,193,673	65,810	29,000	44.1
R.I.	172,373	5,171	1,759	34.0
S.C.	620,711	18,621	2,312	12.4
S.D.	148,080	4,442	400	9.0
Tenn.	841,974	25,259	6,000	23.8
Texas	2,822,754	84,683	N.A.	—
Utah	314,471	9,434	2,086	22.1
Vt.	104,356	3,131	200	6.4
Va.	1,100,723	33,022	25,000	75.7
Wash.	780,730	23,422	1,300	5.6
W.Va.	404,771	12,143	N.A.	—
Wis.	945,337	28,360	1,300	4.6
Wyo.	90,587	2,718	N.A.	—
D.C.	125,848	3,775	N.A.	—
Totals	44,335,000	1,330,050	437,618	

Source: The Council for Exceptional Children   * Estimated   ** Not Available

intelligence tests. The phrase "gifted and talented" was adopted to underscore the switch away from a purely intellectual definition. Today the most widely used definition is the one adopted by the U.S. Office of Education in 1972:

> Gifted and talented children are those identified by professionally qualified persons who by virtue of outstanding abilities are capable of high performance. . . . Children capable of high performance include those with demonstrated achievement and/or potential ability in any of the following areas, singly or in combination: (1) general intellectual ability, (2) specific academic aptitude, (3) creative or productive thinking, (4) leadership ability, (5) visual and performing arts, and (6) psychomotor ability.

Increased Commitments; Continuing Problems

During the past seven years the fortunes of gifted children have been on the rise. To help meet the special educational needs of this group, the Office of Education in 1972 created the Office of Gifted and Talented. The 1974 amendments to the Elementary and Secondary Education Act include "the first substantive authority for support of the special education of the nation's gifted and talented children."[7] In fiscal 1976, the first year in which the provision became effective, $2.3 million in federal funds were spent on gifted programs. By the following year the federal allocation had risen to $5.6 million. More help is on the way. The Gifted and Talented Children's Education Act of 1978, enacted by Congress last October, increased the authorization for federal spending on the gifted to $25 million in fiscal 1979 (the year ending Sept. 30), $30 million in fiscal 1980, $35 million in fiscal 1981, $40 million in fiscal 1982 and $50 million in fiscal 1983.

State governments also have increased their commitments to special education for the gifted and talented in recent years. In 1971, only 21 states had legislation pertaining to the education of gifted children. As of June 1, 1977, according to a survey conducted for the U.S. Office of Education by the Council for Exceptional Children, 43 states had some type of written policy governing programs and services for the gifted; 18 states had an officially adopted state plan for the education of gifted and talented youth; 25 states reported that their state plans were "being developed" or had been developed but not "officially" adopted.[8]

---

[7] Council for Exceptional Children, *Public Policy and the Education of Exceptional Children* (1976), p. 136.

[8] Council for Exceptional Children, "The Nation's Commitment to the Education of Gifted and Talented Children and Youth: Summary of Findings from a 1977 Survey of States and Territories," April 1978, p. 13.

Largest Allocation of State Funds
for Gifted Children, 1976-77

Rank	State	1976-77 State Funds	% of Total 1976-77 State Funds of Reporting States
1	California	$15,570,000	27.66%
2	Florida	15,500,000	27.53
3	North Carolina	8,100,000	14.39
4	Georgia	4,200,000	7.46
5	Connecticut	3,000,000	5.33
6	Illinois	2,600,000	4.62
7	Virginia	1,400,000	2.49
8	Missouri	1,300,000	2.31
	Totals	$51,670,000	91.8 %*

* Figures do not add to total because of rounding.
Source: The Council for Exceptional Children

The states spent over $56 million on gifted and talented education in 1977. In 27 states, at least one full-time person worked on gifted and talented programs that year; in 14 other states there was a part-time person. In 1971, only 24 states had a position with designated responsibilities for gifted and talented educational services; only 10 of the 24 states assigned persons to gifted programs for half of their time or more.

Although the status of gifted and talented children has significantly improved since the early 1970s, educational efforts on behalf of this group still have "a long way to go to achieve parity with other educational programs," the Council for Exceptional Children concluded in its recent report to the U.S. Office of Education. The council listed the following statistics to back up its conclusion:

Only 32 states did or could report the number of gifted and talented children receiving special services during 1976-77. Only eight of these states provided services to over half of their potential gifted and talented school-age populations.

Although there has been an increase in state personnel designated to work in gifted and talented programs, there were only 11 states that had more than the equivalent of one full-time person. Ten states had less than a half-time equivalent in 1976-77; four of those states had no one at all.

Over 65 percent of the federal allocation for gifted and talented programs in 1976-77 was used by only 10 states.

No data was forthcoming that demonstrated the aptness or effectiveness of the present services to the gifted and talented.

"Gifted and talented children are still facing the problem of educational neglect. . .," the council concluded. "The conditions identified five years ago as deterrents are still operative — lack of adequate funding from both federal and state coffers; lack of trained personnel assigned to work with programs for gifted and talented; lack of sufficient training opportunities for those who want to improve their skills; lack of substantiated procedures for identifying gifted and talented children. . .; lack of adequate information in program effectiveness not only with the gifted and talented in general but particularly with special subpopulations; and lack of information from and to all levels of this important enterprise."

Recognition of Gifted Kids' Special Needs

The new wave of interest in the educational needs of America's brightest youngsters is attributed in part to parental pressure. "Parents have seen money spent on the disadvantaged, the handicapped, the children who don't speak English. They haven't seen it spent on the gifted, and they're beginning to ask why," explained Isabelle Rucker, director of Virginia's Office of Exceptional Children.[9]

Prompted by lawsuits such as the one filed by the Illinois couple, school administrators are increasingly becoming convinced that failure to provide classes for gifted students may be as "discriminatory" an action as failure to provide instruction for other exceptional children. "It's simply not equitable that we appropriate millions of dollars for the handicapped and do nothing or almost nothing for the exceptionally bright student. . .," said Roger Ming, superintendent of education for the gifted for the New York State Department of Education. "What we've really got to do is provide for the needs of all our students and their various abilities."[10]

The best argument for special education for the gifted, its supporters say, is the mounting evidence that bright youngsters do not necessarily thrive without special attention. Many are so discouraged by regular classroom instruction that they never fulfill their potential. A few become so bored and frustrated that they drop out of school. Their plight was described by Sidney P. Marland Jr., who was then U.S. commissioner of education, in a report to Congress issued in March 1972. "We are increasingly being stripped of the comfortable notion that a bright mind will make it on its own," Marland wrote. "Intellectual and creative talent cannot survive educational neglect and apathy."

---

[9] Quoted in *Newsweek*, Oct. 23, 1978, p. 111.

[10] Quoted in *The New York Times*, March 19, 1978.

According to a recent estimate, perhaps as many as three-fourths of all potentially gifted and talented persons do not attain the educational levels of which they are capable.[11] Inexperienced teachers often fail to recognize or misinterpret a child's exceptional or unusual abilities. Insensitive classmates can make gifted children miserable by labeling them "freaks" or "eggheads." "We hadn't realized until recently that giftedness is a kind of handicap," said Ted Rifkin, chairman of the English department at New York City's Bronx High School of Science. "Bright kids need a structured and challenging environment just as much as deaf kids need an atmosphere sensitive to their special needs."[12]

Current Programs: Enrichment, Acceleration

Educators are trying to meet the educational needs of gifted and talented children in a variety of ways. What these programs have in common is an attempt to stimulate creativity, allow in-depth exploration of a subject and encourage progress according to interest and ability, not age. Those selected for Virginia's "Governor's School," four-week sessions for gifted children at three Virginia colleges, take courses ranging from Asian studies and physics to drama and dance. The University of South Alabama offers special Saturday classes for bright youths taught by college students who are working on degrees in gifted child education. The State of Illinois has established regional centers to assist communities in planning and carrying out programs.

Three basic methods for better education of the gifted have been widely employed in American schools: (1) acceleration, which speeds the rapid learner through the grades, (2) enrichment, which keeps him at the normal rate of promotion but gives him additional study material and additional "learning experiences," and (3) ability grouping, which puts bright children in special sections for harder work than is expected of other pupils. "There really isn't one approach that works better than the other for all situations," according to John Grossi of the Council for Exceptional Children. "You can't make a blanket statement and say that acceleration is the best approach or enrichment is the best approach. It all depends on the individual child and the individual environment in which the child is operating."

Acceleration was the favored technique for the exceptionally able child early in the century. Skipping a grade was the reward of fast learning. Acceleration later fell into disfavor. Many educators felt that a gifted child was put at a disadvantage when placed with children who were physically larger and socially and

---

[11] Maynard C. Reynolds and Jack W. Birch, *Teaching Exceptional Children in All America's Schools* (1977), p. 198.
[12] Quoted in *Newsweek*, Oct. 23, 1978, p. 111.

emotionally more mature. Skipping grades proved a handicap also when the gifted child skipped an important step in acquisition of skills. It then came to be considered preferable to keep the fast learner with his age group and give him an "enriched" curriculum. While other children continued with drill and repetition of a lesson, the gifted child would be reading, working on other projects, or participating in some activity that would widen or deepen his understanding of the course subject.

Moderate acceleration has gained fresh support in recent years. For the most part, however, acceleration is achieved today, not by skipping grades, but by introducing certain subjects at lower educational levels than formerly. The College Board Advanced Placement Program, which gives college credit for special courses in high school, is an example of combining the existing school program with acceleration and curriculum enrichment.

The leading proponent of acceleration is Dr. Julian C. Stanley, director of the "Study of Mathematically Precocious Youth" at Johns Hopkins University in Baltimore. Each year Dr. Stanley and his associates ask teachers in Maryland and surrounding states to nominate seventh graders who are extremely advanced in mathematics. The youngsters are given the Scholastic Aptitude Test for math, normally used for college admissions purposes. The test results are used to identify students ready to do college work. Most of the children identified as "mathematically precocious" do not go directly to college. The overwhelming majority remain in regular schools and take classes at Johns Hopkins on Saturdays and during the summer. Last year Johns Hopkins started a similar program for verbally gifted youths. Over 50 youngsters identified by the verbal portion of the Scholastic Aptitude Test participated in the Saturday and summer programs.

Last year 17 students aged 10 to 16 were enrolled in a special early entrance program at the University of Washington in Seattle. Overall they did remarkably well, maintaining a Phi Beta Kappa level 3.6 grade point average, compared with a 2.8 average for all university students. Despite the obvious social and dating problems, most of the youngsters seem to adjust well to college life. Child psychologist Halbert Robinson, who set up the program in 1977, met with them as a group twice a week. "These kids have gone through their young lives thought of by peers and even by some parents as a little weird," Robinson explained. "But when they come here and find others like themselves, they don't just thrive. They blossom."[13]

---

[13] Quoted in *Newsweek*, June 11, 1979, p. 113.

History of the Gifted Movement

INTEREST in the education of gifted children goes back to ancient times. Plato speculated upon ways of telling which children were gifted so that they might be educated for leadership in the state. In *The Republic*, the Greek philosopher said children should be trained for whatever their abilities suited them, regardless of their social class. He was convinced that Greek democracy could be no better than its leadership, and he wished to educate superior youths for this important task.

The Romans later adopted some of Plato's ideas and gave special training to gifted youths so that they might become leaders in war, oratory and government. Charlemagne, the Frankish King (768-814), advocated the education at public expense of promising children among the common people. In the 16th century, the Turkish sultan Suleiman the Magnificent founded a school for gifted youth in Constantinople. Emissaries spread throughout the Ottoman Empire selecting the fairest, strongest and brightest boys without regard to family background. Comenius, the 17th century Czech religious leader and educational reformer, made frequent references to students with unusual aptitude for learning and advocated financial aid for bright students from poor homes.

Similar ideas were expressed a century later by Thomas Jefferson. It was imperative, Jefferson wrote in 1779, for those "whom nature hath endowed with genius and virtue" to be educated for public service, so that they might be "worthy to receive, and able to guard the sacred deposit of the rights and liberties of their fellow citizens." In his "Notes on the State of Virginia," Jefferson proposed strengthening "the natural aristocracy of virtues and talents" by the establishment of rigorously selective tests in the grammar schools through which "the best geniuses will be raked from the rubbish annually."

A number of schools, usually stimulated by a dynamic or assertive educator, introduced special programs for gifted children after the Civil War. One of the earliest attempts to provide for gifted children in the public schools was begun in 1869 by William T. Harris, superintendent of the St. Louis public school system. Harris' plan allowed gifted children to accelerate at their own pace rather than remaining in the "lock-step" program. The fact that this pioneer plan was not widely used "suggests that, even then, educators were nervous about making separate arrangements for the gifted and talented."[14]

---

[14] Gallagher and Weiss, *op. cit.*, pp. 12-13. See also Gertrude H. Hildreth's *Introduction to the Gifted* (1966).

In the late 19th and early 20th centuries, the most common method for coping with diversity of abilities and achievement among students in public schools was multiple tracking: the establishment of fast, medium and slow groups. One of the first multiple tracking programs in the nation was established in Elizabeth, N.J., in 1866. In Cambridge, Mass., the Double Track Plan, set up in 1910, provided parallel courses in the elementary grades — eight years for average students, six years for superior children. According to Gallagher and Weiss: "There is little evidence that these placements resulted in major changes in course content. They were devices to allow students to proceed more rapidly through the existing curriculum than was possible in most conventional arrangements, and to reduce the diversity of student performance faced by the teacher in a single classroom."

A variety of programs designed to individualize instruction and provide for bright students emerged during the first quarter of the 20th century. A survey by the U.S. Bureau of Education[15] in 1911 found 6 percent of the U.S. cities reporting special classes for gifted pupils. Rapid-advancement classes for bright students appeared in New York City and Worcester, Mass., as early as 1901. Frederick Burke established a self-instruction plan for superior students in San Francisco in 1912. A similar program was set up by one of his associates, Dr. Carlton Washburne, in Winnetka, Ill., in 1920. The following year, Cleveland, Ohio, established one of the most ambitious programs. Called the Major Work Classes, it emphasized enrichment, special curricula and acceleration of course content rather than merely on speeding youngsters through a standard curriculum.

Intelligence Testing; Work of L. M. Terman

Educators at the turn of the century were intensely interested in the suggestion that mental capacity could be mathematically measured, but they lacked an acceptable instrument for measuring it. A French psychologist, Alfred Binet, was the first to create an effective measuring device. Binet and an assistant, Theodore Simon, developed a series of graded tests to determine the ability of children to meet the demands of primary education. The Binet test, first published in 1905, was used primarily to identify youngsters who were mentally retarded.[16]

American psychologist Lewis M. Terman, a professor of psychology and education at Stanford University, published a

---

[15] The Office of Education, established in 1867, became the Bureau of Education in 1870 and retained that name until 1929, when it again became the Office of Education.

[16] See "Educational Testing," *E.R.R.*, 1958 Vol. II, pp. 933-951, and "Human Intelligence," *E.R.R.*, 1969 Vol. II, pp. 615-632.

"The Creator has withheld from Man the shark's teeth, the bird's wings, the elephant's trunk and the hound's or horse's racing feet. The creative power planted in a minority of mankind has to do duty for all the marvelous physical assets that are built into every specimen of Man's non-human fellow creatures. If society fails to make the most of this one human asset, or if, worse still, it perversely sets itself to stifle it, Man is throwing away his birthright of being the Lord of creation and is condemning himself to be, instead, the least effective species on the face of this planet."

Arnold Toynbee*

*"Is America Neglecting Her Creative Minority?" in *Widening Horizons in Creativity* (1964), C. W. Taylor, ed.

revised version of the Binet test in 1916. The Stanford-Binet Individual Test of Intelligence, as it was called, played an important role in subsequent programs for the gifted and it served as the basic tool for the inclusion of youngsters in the longitudinal study of giftedness conducted by Terman and his associates, starting in 1921. He selected 1,500 California youngsters whose IQ's were over 140 and studied their development for 35 years.

Terman's findings dispelled many myths about gifted children. He and his colleagues reported that contrary to popular thought, gifted children were not physically, retarded, unsocial misfits. On the whole, the gifted children studied by Terman were healthier and more stable emotionally than the average child. "The deviation of the gifted" from the general population "is in the upward direction for nearly all traits," Terman wrote. "There is no law of compensation whereby the intellectual superiority of the gifted tends to be offset by inferiorities along non-intellectual lines." Although most of the Terman youngsters fulfilled their early promise, "a good many failed to achieve in proportion to their intellectual ability." This was due in large part, Terman wrote, to "the absence of educational procedures adapted to children of exceptional ability."[17]

Interest in Gifted Spurred by Sputnik

Interest in the gifted child grew after World War II as the baby boom generation reached school age. But the spectacular Russian "firsts" in space, beginning with Sputnik in 1957, provided the real impetus. They aroused and alarmed the American public who, unfairly or not, blamed the schools for America's second-best status. From all sides came demands for higher standards, more training in science, mathematics and foreign languages, better provisions for bright students and harder study for all.

The Eisenhower administration responded by proposing federal aid to strengthen teaching facilities — particularly in science and math — and to increase educational opportunities for talented students. Congress assented by passing the National Defense Education Act of 1958 — a $1 billion program geared basically to science, mathematics and foreign language instruction. It also included funds for new instructional equipment, such as language laboratories, and extended financial aid to college students, particularly future teachers.

In the late 1950s and early 1960s the "pursuit of excellence" became a rallying cry for American educators. Schools hastened to examine their curriculums and academic requirements. Programs for gifted students were introduced on a wide scale. A national conference on the academically talented secondary school student, sponsored by the National Education Association, met in Washington in February 1958. The conference, under the chairmanship of James B. Conant, president emeritus of Harvard, drew up a number of recommendations for activating gifted-child programs in the public schools.

---

[17] Lewis M. Terman and Melita H. Oden, "The Stanford Studies of the Gifted" in *The Gifted Child* (1951), edited by Paul Witty, pp. 24, 45.

During this period the number of research projects on the nature of giftedness increased significantly. "Probably 20 times as much material was published on this subject in the decade 1950-1960 as in any previous 10-year period," Gertrude H. Hildreth wrote. Among the works published during the 1950s was *The Gifted Group at Mid-Life* (1959) by Lewis M. Terman and Melita H. Oden. This was the fifth volume published as a result of the "Genetic Studies of Genius" project launched by Terman in 1921.[18]

The impact of the National Defense Education Act and other programs for the gifted was short-lived, according to the current director of the Office of Gifted and Talented, Dorothy A. Sisk. "The majority of these programs did not have a lasting effect on education provisions for the gifted," she wrote, "and educational program development for gifted and talented was sporadic and not widespread."[19]

Growth of Federal Involvement and Funding

In the mid-1960s the attention of American educators was drawn increasingly to the problems of disadvantaged youths. Billions of dollars were pumped into programs to compensate minority youngsters for the shortcomings of their environment and to ensure "equality of educational opportunity." Much of this funding was provided by the Elementary and Secondary Education Act of 1965 — the first general aid-to-education program ever adopted by Congress. During the next decade, ESEA coverage gradually was expanded to include other special groups, including non-English-speaking children,[20] handicapped children,[21] children with learning disabilities and the gifted.

Although the problems of gifted children received no priority in the late 1960s, they were not entirely forgotten. A White House task force on education for the gifted was established by President Johnson in 1967. The 1969 amendments to the Elementary and Secondary Act included a number of provisions pertaining to gifted children. The amendments authorized the U.S. commissioner of education to make grants to state education agencies to provide services and assistance to local school districts for programs for gifted and talented youngsters.

---

[18] Earlier works were *The Mental and Physical Traits of a Thousand Gifted Children* (1925) by Terman et al; *The Early Mental Traits of Three Hundred Geniuses* (1926) by Catherine M. Cox; *The Promise of Youth* (1930) by Barbara S. Burks, Dortha Jensen and Terman; and *The Gifted Child Grows Up* (1947) by Terman and Oden. In 1968, 12 years after Terman's death, Melita Oden published a monograph on "The Fulfillment of Promise: 40-Year Follow-up of the Terman Gifted Group."

[19] Dorothy A. Sisk, "Education of the Gifted and Talented: A National Perspective," *Journal for the Education of the Gifted,* February 1978, p. 5.

[20] See "Bilingual Education," *E.R.R.,* 1977 Vol. II, pp. 617-636.

[21] See "Rights of the Handicapped," *E.R.R.,* 1974 Vol. II, pp. 885-904.

The most significant provision in the 1969 amendments, as they pertained to gifted children, was the one directing the commissioner of education to conduct a study to (1) determine the extent to which special educational assistance programs are necessary or useful to meet the needs of gifted and talented children, (2) show which federal programs are being used to meet the needs of gifted children, (3) evaluate how existing programs could be more effectively used to meet those needs, and (4) recommend new programs needed. The study was begun in August 1970 and concluded in June 1971. The findings were published in a report submitted to Congress by the U.S. commissioner of education, Sidney P. Marland Jr., in March 1972.

The Marland report urged the federal government to take the lead in eliminating "the widespread neglect of this population." "Federal leadership in this effort is required to confirm and establish provisions for the gifted and talented as a national priority, and to encourage the states to include this priority in their own planning," the report stated. "The experiences of the disadvantaged and handicapped tell us that little is done systematically for special needy groups until the federal government takes an interest and stimulates action."

Cultural and Sexual Barriers

DESPITE the strides that have been made in recent years in establishing programs for bright and talented students, many still complain that "far too many programs for the gifted . . . are essentially collections of fun-and-games activities [that] lack continuity and show little evidence of developing in a systematic fashion the mental processes that led these children to be identified as gifted."[22]

"One of the challenges of creating a satisfactory learning environment for gifted students," James J. Gallagher and Patricia Weiss wrote, "is to provide program content that will make these changes more than hollow administrative shells or fancy packages in which little happens. . . . The general lack of systematic and suitable curriculum material for the gifted and talented in all subjects remains a tight brake upon new educational adventures. Unless there is substantive work to produce curricula, special programs for the gifted and talented will not

---

[22] Joseph Renzulli, *The Enrichment Triad Model: A Guide for Developing Defensible Programs for the Gifted and Talented* (1977), p. 6.

be interesting and useful to either student or teacher, or acceptable to parents."

Most educators agree on the need to develop better means of identifying gifted and talented children. Despite the general acceptance of the broadened definition of giftedness to include creativity, advanced social skills and exceptional physical aptitude, there remains a strong emphasis on IQ tests and teacher recommendations for identification. "The worst cases in which intelligence is overlooked involve girls and minority students of both sexes," *New York Times* education correspondent Gene Maeroff wrote last year. "Too many teachers are simply biased in their expectations and pay little attention to the traits of these children. Furthermore, cultural prejudices tend to keep girls and minority students from reaching their full intellectual growth, making it that much more of a problem to discern the exceptional promise that may be buried deep within such a child."[23]

Stereotyping Schoolgirls With 'Math Anxiety'

Educators have become more sensitive to the special problems of gifted girls and women in recent years. "Like other minority groups, gifted girls are in dire danger of behaving according to the stereotype constructed for them by the culture," James J. Gallagher wrote in 1975.[24] Evidence abounds that girls are not expected to do as well as boys in mathematics or in the sciences that require a solid understanding of math. "Our society has conditioned people to think of this as male territory," explained Dr. Bernard Miller, director of the Hunter College Elementary School and Hunter High, two schools for gifted children in New York City. "Walk into any advanced math or physics class in the city and you will see five boys to every girl; walk into any advanced language class and the reverse will be true."[25]

Dr. Miller blamed "math anxiety" for the fact that more boys than girls qualify for Hunter High. Those involved in the Johns Hopkins program for the mathematically precocious have found that, consistently, about 25 percent of the seventh grade boys given the math part of the Scholastic Aptitude Test score more than 500 points out of a possible 800. Only 12 percent of the seventh grade girls given the test do as well.[26]

One view of the changes necessary in order for gifted girls to receive full opportunities in math and science is to alter the sex-

---

[23] Gene Maeroff, "Smart Kids Have Problems Too," *Parents' Magazine,* September 1978, pp. 72-73.

[24] James J. Gallagher, *Teaching the Gifted Child* (1975), p. 48.

[25] Quoted by Pat McNees Mancini in "School for Whiz Kids," *New York,* Nov. 14, 1977, p. 76.

[26] See Cynthia Parsons' "Challenging Intellectually Gifted Math Pupils," *The Christian Science Monitor,* May 21, 1979.

role stereotyping that leads parents and educators to have different expectations for girls and boys, particularly in mathematical achievement and professional goals. It will also be necessary to modify the sex-role stereotypes held by educators and the adolescent peer group that discourage female creativity, intellectual risk taking and achievement.[27]

Search for Gifted Minority-Group Children

The problems of identifying gifted minority-group youths long have been of concern to educators. Often these youngsters are overlooked because their behavior patterns and responses vary from the typical indicators of giftedness, such as high IQ scores or proficiency in the dominant language. "When the behavior of culturally diverse gifted and talented children is interpreted, their boredom with already learned or irrelevant material is often interpreted as anti-intellectual," Mary M. Frasier wrote in a paper prepared for the Council for Exceptional Children. "Dissatisfaction expressed as disruptive or impulsive behavior reinforces misperceptions. The desire to accept challenges may be seen as aggressive or unrealistic."[28]

Dorothy Sisk of the Office of Gifted and Talented has noted that many inner-city school administrators are so fearful of low scores on IQ tests that they hesitate to test children. "Or if they do," she added, "they may be reluctant to give up their star students to a special program."[29] A background paper on gifted children that was circulated recently within the U.S. Office of Education stated: "With the heavy emphasis on remedial education for inner-city youngsters and budget problems that appear insurmountable, it is rare that inner-city school officials expend effort on either identifying disadvantaged inner-city gifted or establishing programs for these children."[30]

New techniques for discovering gifted minority youth are being developed. One that is frequently mentioned is the System of Multicultural Pluralistic Assessment,[31] developed by Jane R. Mercer, a professor of sociology at the Riverside campus of the University of California. SOMPA employs a way of cal-

---

[27] See Lynn Fox, "Sex Differences: Implications for Program Planning for the Academically Gifted," *The Gifted and the Creative: A Fifty-year Perspective,* ed., Julian C. Stanley et al. (1977), pp. 113-138.

[28] "The Culturally Diverse Gifted and Talented Child," paper produced for the Office of Gifted and Talented, U.S. Office of Education, by the Council for Exceptional Children, May 1978.

[29] Quoted in *Newsweek,* Oct. 23, 1978, p. 108.

[30] Quoted by Maeroff, *op. cit.,* p. 73.

[31] See Jane R. Mercer and June F. Lewis, "Using the System of Multicultural Pluralistic Assessment (SOMPA) to Identify the Gifted Minority Child," in "Educational Planning for the Gifted: Overcoming Cultural, Geographic, and Socioeconomic Barriers," edited by Alexinia Y. Baldwin, Gayle Haywood Gear and Leonard J. Lucito, Council for Exceptional Children (1978), pp. 7-14.

culating a student's estimated learning potential by using national and ethnic comparisons.

E. Paul Torrance, a professor of educational psychology at the University of Georgia who has worked extensively with disadvantaged black children in the southeastern states, uses group games, role playing, sociodrama, visual arts, creative movement, dance, dramatics, storytelling, creative writing, music and creative problem solving to help identify gifted black children. "If educators are really interested in identifying gifted and talented students in minority groups," Torrance wrote, "they will direct their searches to those characteristics that are valued by the particular minority groups. . . . [F]ew of our standardized tests assess characteristics valued by minority groups. . . ."[32]

"The problem of providing adequately for disadvantaged gifted students is far more than one of ignoring the existence of talent from different environments," Torrance wrote in an earlier article. "It cannot be solved simply by identifying and inserting them into existing programs for gifted and talented children. . . . Successful programs will have to be special to some degree in content of the curriculum, methods of instruction and the learning environment to be used."[33]

Many educators believe that programs for gifted students will benefit all children. Because numerous techniques now applied to education of the gifted may be adapted to education of average students, the emphasis on gifted children may eventually strengthen educational programs in general. "Ultimately, the gifted movement is going to raise the standards of teaching in our whole society," declared Dr. Joseph Carbone, a principal in Westchester County, N.Y. "And isn't that what our American education system is all about?"[34]

It will be difficult to expand programs for gifted children until Americans resolve their conflicting feelings about their most talented young citizens. Those who support these programs argue that, without them, the country risks shortchanging the development of its future leadership. Many people believe this is a risk Americans cannot afford to take.

---

[32] E. Paul Torrance, "Ways of Discovering Gifted Black Children," in "Educational Planning for the Gifted. . ." *op. cit.,* pp. 29-30.

[33] E. Paul Torrance, "Creatively Gifted and Disadvantaged Gifted Students," in *The Gifted and the Creative: A Fifty Year Perspective* (1977), p. 192.

[34] Quoted in *The New York Times,* March 19, 1978.

Selected Bibliography

Books

Dennis, Wayne and Margaret W. Dennis, *The Intellectually Gifted: An Overview*, Grune & Stratton, 1976.

Barbe, Walter B. and Joseph S. Renzulli, *Psychology and Education of the Gifted*, John Wiley and Sons, 1975.

Gallagher, James J., *Teaching the Gifted Child*, 2nd ed., Allyn and Bacon, 1975.

Ginsberg, Gina and Charles H. Harrison, *How to Help Your Gifted Child: A Handbook for Parents and Teachers*, Monarch Press, 1977.

Newland, T. Ernest, *The Gifted in Socioeducational Perspective*, Prentice-Hall, 1976.

Sanderlin, Owenita, *Teaching Gifted Children*, A. S. Barnes and Co., 1973.

Stanley, Julian C. et al., eds., *The Gifted and the Creative: A Fifty Year Perspective*, Johns Hopkins University Press, 1977.

Articles

Bentsen, Cheryl, "The Brightest Kids," *New York*, June 18, 1979.

Maeroff, Gene, "Smart Kids Have Problems Too," *Parents' Magazine*, September 1978.

—— "The Unfavored Gifted Few," *The New York Times Magazine*, Aug. 21, 1977.

Mancini, Pat McNees, "School for Whiz Kids," *New York*, Nov. 14, 1977.

Mitchell, Patricia and Donald Erickson, "The Education of Gifted and Talented Children," *Exceptional Children*, September 1978.

Seligmann, Jean, "When Kids of 10 Go Off to College," *Newsweek*, June 11, 1979.

Sheils, Merrill, "The Gifted Child," *Newsweek*, Oct. 23, 1978.

"Was the Kid Too Smart to Learn?" *Time*, April 23, 1979.

Reports and Studies

Baldwin, Alexinia Y. et al., eds., "Educational Planning for the Gifted: Overcoming Cultural, Geographic and Socioeconomic Barriers," Council for Exceptional Children, 1978.

Council for Exceptional Children, "The Nation's Commitment to the Education of Gifted and Talented Children and Youth; Summary of Findings from a 1977 Survey of States and Territories," April 1978.

Editorial Research Reports, "Education of Gifted Children," 1959 Vol. II, pp. 793; "Educational Testing," 1958 Vol. II, p. 931; "Elite vs. Mass Education," 1958 Vol. I, p. 341; "Human Intelligence," 1969 Vol. II, p. 615.

Gallagher, James J. and Patricia Weiss, "The Education of Gifted and Talented Students: A History and Prospectus," Council for Basic Education, 1979.

Kaplan, Sandra N., "Providing Programs for the Gifted and Talented: A Handbook," National/State Leadership Training Institute on the Gifted and the Talented, February 1977.

PRIVATE SCHOOL RESURGENCE

by

William V. Thomas

Apr. 20
1 9 7 9

PRIVATE SCHOOL RESURGENCE

ONCE THOUGHT of as a luxury few families could afford, a private education is coming to be considered a middle-class necessity. Many parents who might otherwise have sent their children to public elementary and secondary schools as a matter of course are now enrolling them in private schools. The new interest in private education is largely the result of growing dissatisfaction over the declining standards of achievement and discipline reported in the nation's public school systems. Traditionally, private institutions have stressed high academic requirements and instruction in moral values, qualities some parents believe are not emphasized enough in the public classrooms.

The shortcomings of public schools, particularly inner-city schools, have been widely publicized, as have the advantages of good schooling to qualify students for admission to college. Although relatively few Americans have had much contact with private schools, the general assumption is that they are superior to public schools. And in recent years, more families than in the past have seemed willing to pay high tuitions in the hope that private education will give their college-bound children the added encouragement to excel.

The U.S. Office of Education estimated that last fall there were 47.8 million elementary and secondary school children in the country. Out of that number, five million, or about 10 percent, went to private schools. While public school enrollments nationwide are dropping at an annual rate of around 2 percent, private school attendance has increased steadily — last year by slightly over 1 percent.

Some religious schools have gained in enrollment as a result of the apparent movement away from public education. Suburban Jewish day schools have attracted an increasing number of students, while Christian-oriented private academies have proliferated throughout the southern states. Catholic schools, after a period of decline, have also begun to grow. It is estimated that of the five million students now attending private schools, over four million are in church-directed schools — the vast majority in Catholic parochial schools.[1] Other private schools, which prefer the name "independent" schools, account for the

[1] The National Center for Educational Statistics reports the following school enrollments in the 1978-79 year: Catholic parochial schools, 3.3 million; Lutheran schools, 202,000; Baptist, 151,000; Jewish, 81,000; and Quaker, 15,000.

remaining million or so students. The number is not known precisely. The 825 member schools of the National Association of Independent Schools (NAIS) have a combined enrollment of 750,000. Educational authorities believe other independent schools account for about a quarter-million students.

Despite their new popularity, private schools face a host of problems. Perhaps the biggest of these is with the federal government. The Internal Revenue Service wants to revoke the tax-exempt status of private schools that cannot meet racial guidelines the agency is seeking to impose. This action springs from the founding of "white" or "Christian" academies in many southern communities as their public schools were desegregated. But many other private schools fear, for one reason or another, that their tax status might also be jeopardized, and they are urging Congress to block the guidelines.

No one knows how many applicants are turned away from private schools every year. But it is certain that the demand for admission far exceeds the availability of places. Some of the more prestigious New England academies reject as many as 95 percent of those who apply. Sometimes prospective students are refused for academic reasons, sometimes for lack of space. Existing institutions treasure their small-school character and hence are not eager to undertake sizable expansion. However, the exclusivity of many private schools — one of their principal attractions — leaves them vulnerable to criticism of imposing racial barriers.

Loss of Confidence in the Public Schools

Parents are likely to find private schools as costly as colleges. It is not uncommon for a day student to pay $2,000 a year tuition; some boarding schools charge as much as $6,000. These expenses to the parents are in addition to local school taxes, which all property owners must pay regardless of whether their children attend private or public schools.

Why are parents willing to spend so much for their children to forgo public schooling? Donald Barr, former headmaster of the Dalton School in New York City, said that "most of our students [came to us] because their parents felt they had no other place to go." They "are not running from integration . . . and crime. [They] are just unhappy with the public schools," Barr said. This sense of dissatisfaction was confirmed by a *New York Times* poll. Of 3,500 suburban New York residents questioned, nearly half said they either had no or very little confidence in public education. Public schools ranked eighth in a list of what the respondents said they liked most about their communities.[2]

---

[2] The poll, conducted in 1978, was cited in *The New York Times*, March 23, 1979, which also quoted Barr.

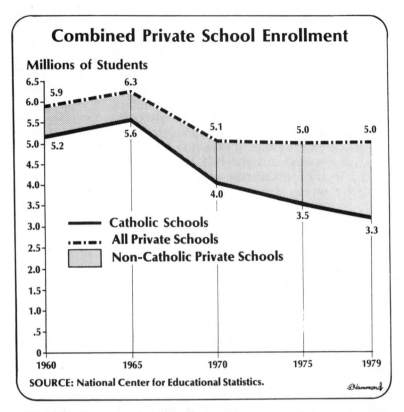

Combined Private School Enrollment

Millions of Students

- —— Catholic Schools
- ·—·—· All Private Schools
- ▓ Non-Catholic Private Schools

1960 · 1965 · 1970 · 1975 · 1979

SOURCE: National Center for Educational Statistics.

The NAIS reported in February it expects the trend away from public education to increase, partly because of the many loan and deferred-payment plans adopted by schools to attract more youngsters from middle-income families. Independent schools have also established special financial aid programs intended to increase enrollment of minority students. Thomas Wilcox, a spokesman for the association, said in an interview that applications are up nationwide 10 to 60 percent, "and in the Northeast it is all but a deluge." The increase, he said, "is a lot more than schools can handle."

Independent schools do not usually lower their standards to meet the demand for admission, so in most cases a rise in attendance has meant a costly expansion of facilities. A number of eastern schools with large endowments for years have tried to assemble "democratic" student bodies. St. Paul's (497 students, $46 million endowment), Groton (300 students, $21 million), Deerfield (558, $21 million), Lawrenceville (700, $24 million), Hotchkiss (478, $10.4 million) and Choate (920, $11.7 million) regularly seek a wide range of students. But inflation and limited resources, officials contend, rather than "any residue of social snobbery,"[3] keep them from reaching farther.

[3] *Time* magazine, June 5, 1978, p. 50.

According to the Office of Education, one of every 10 white students in the South is now enrolled in a segregated private school. In many instances these schools — often called academies and sometimes "Christian academies" — came into being in the early days of desegregation to circumvent federal civil rights legislation. U.S. tax laws grant income-tax deductions for donations to eligible non-profit institutions, and at present these schools are on the eligibility list that is drawn up by the Internal Revenue Service. But the IRS has proposed new regulations which, if they ultimately are put into effect, would deny eligibility to any private school that — by IRS definition — practices racial discrimination. Spokesmen for private schools say that without the tax exemption, hundreds of private schools, and not just in the South, might be forced to close.

Tax Ruling Against Segregated Academies

Defining just what constitutes racial discrimination is the sticking point. Since it first proposed the regulations last August, the agency has received over 100,000 complaints about them. This opposition extends to Congress, where several bills have been introduced to block or revise the IRS proposals *(see p. 144)*. Much of the congressional opposition arises in the South, but by no means is confined to that region. Private schools throughout the country, portraying themselves as innocent bystanders, fear they will be ensnared in the net of regulations the IRS has devised for segregated academies. However, there are degrees of opposition among the private schools. Generally, the long-established schools have misgivings about the rules but have not been nearly as outspoken as those operated by evangelical Christians.

At the heart of the controversy is a provision that would automatically question the tax-exempt status of any private school set up or expanded after the desegregation of local public schools, if it does not enroll a significant number of blacks or other minority students. The IRS has said it will specifically review the tax-exempt status of two categories of private schools: (1) those (there are about 20) that have been found by the courts to have engaged in discrimination but which still receive tax exemptions, and (2) predominantly white schools which were established, or those whose enrollments grew by more than 10 percent, in the period after court-ordered school desegregation. But both groups would receive a hearing. Schools in the second group could attempt to prove to the IRS that they did not practice discrimination. Those in the first group could attempt to show that the courts' findings were no longer valid.

The simplest way for a school to satisfy IRS requirements would be to enroll a sufficient number of minority students.

Under the proposed regulations, any "reviewable" school found to have a percentage of minority students equal to one-fifth of the percentage of minority students in the surrounding community would retain its ranking as a tax-exempt institution. John Estey of NAIS testified that many well-intentioned private schools would have great difficulty fulfilling the 20 percent requirement. "Roughly 200 boarding schools in our association draw students from all over the country and it is a major task to define the communities served and then ascertain minority school-age population in those communities."[4]

To the IRS, the regulations are a matter of enforcing what the courts have commanded it to do *(see p. 148)* in helping to fulfill the national commitment to racial equality. But some school officials say the regulations, if applied, would declare them guilty until they proved their innocence. Some of the schools with a strong religious orientation fear that the IRS, in its action, is taking a step toward federal control of religious principles. "You can't even be a religion now without the approval of the IRS," Eugene McCarthy, the former Minnesota senator and presidential candidate, said recently. "In medieval times you set up a board to determine who the heretics were. Now the IRS does it."[5]

Debate Over IRS Test for Discrimination

"If ever there was an example of the 'new despotism,' it is the Internal Revenue Service's proposed non-discrimination guidelines," wrote John Lofton Jr., editor of the conservative publication *Battle Line.*[6] Critics of the regulations say the IRS has neither the need nor the authority to establish new rules in this area. No one defends tax breaks for segregated schools. But opponents argue that the IRS already has ways to take action against schools where there is real evidence of discrimination. Opponents have also claimed that the IRS lacks the legal standing to make important rules on such controversial matters without direction from Congress. "The IRS aren't the people to do this," Lofton wrote. "Congress has said nothing — [IRS officials] should not look solely to the courts for justification."

"The schools are placed under a presumption of guilt and would have to prove themselves innocent," Jack Clayton, spokesman for the American Association of Christian Schools,[7] told Editorial Research Reports. The IRS responds that the regulations are grounded in the court's repeated affirmation of the "badge of doubt" concept, that private schools could be

---

[4] Testimony at Internal Revenue Service hearing, Dec. 5, 1978.

[5] Quoted in *The Center Magazine,* March-April 1979, p. 70.

[6] *Battle Line,* December 1978, p. 3.

[7] The association, based in Washington, serves the interests of some 1,200 elementary and secondary schools through the country.

placed in question solely because of the situations in which they were established. "The principle of putting the burden of proof on the schools is inescapable," remarked Mark Wineck, a staff assistant to the House Ways and Means Committee.

After a flood of protests, many of them voiced at a hearing conducted in February by the Ways and Means Subcommittee on Oversight, IRS modified its initial proposals. While keeping its "20 percent test," it did away with a long list of affirmative action requirements.[8] In their place, the agency offered a series of guidelines for local IRS agents to follow in determining whether a particular school discriminates. The guidelines took into account such things as whether the school was formed by a religious group without a significant number of racial minority members — thus protecting Jewish and Amish schools, for example, which had no realistic chance of recruiting black students.

Although the revisions succeeded in muting some of the earlier complaints, they provoked opposition in civil rights groups, which want stronger requirements. Civil rights legal experts argued before the Oversight Subcommittee that the new regulations would weaken anti-discrimination enforcement by removing the underlying assumption in the original proposals: that private schools under review had the burden of proof to show that they were not discriminating.

One fundamental difference between supporters and defenders of the IRS rules is whether tax exemptions are rights which the government is bound to respect, or privileges which the government can confer or deny according to national policy. The great fear of the evangelical schools is that, if the tax breaks are counted as federal assistance, then perhaps the government will assume the right to demand compliance on other rules that apply to schools receiving direct aid. Clayton spoke, for example, of differences between some religious sentiments and government policy on such matters as women's rights and moral conduct.

IRS backers respond that government involvement in school racial policies will not set a precedent in other areas. They argue that the courts have made it clear that the goal of ending racial discrimination is such a central state interest as to be in an entirely different category from other concerns.

Several bills relating to the tax status of private schools have been introduced in Congress since the February hearing. One bill, submitted by Rep. Philip M. Crane, R-Ill., would simply prohibit the IRS from implementing new regulations until after

---

[8] See "Affirmative Action Under Attack," *E.R.R.*, 1979 Vol. I, pp. 225-244.

1980. Other such proposals would permanently ban implementation. Another approach, offered by Rep. Bill Chappell Jr., D-Fla., would allow the IRS to remove a school's tax exemption only if it had been found by a court to be discriminatory. A more far-reaching proposal, introduced by Rep. Robert K. Dornan, R-Calif., would provide that tax-exempt status for private schools and other charitable institutions not be considered federal assistance. The bills have been sent to Ways and Means, but the committee has not acted on them.

Education and Social Change

THOUGH American private schools have existed since colonial times, most of them date only from the 19th century. For decades before the Civil War, the dominant educational institution in the nation was the private academy, usually a boarding school offering both academic and practical courses leading to careers in business or trade.[9] By 1850, there were 6,000 such academies enrolling a quarter-million students. But in the second half of the century, academies began to give way to public schools. At some point in the 1880s, the balance of enrollment tipped from private to public, and the great expansion thereafter was in the public sector.[10]

As the free school proliferated, however, there was a new growth of private schools that differed from the older-style boarding academies. President Richard Henry Jesse of the University of Missouri described the difference in 1892: "The chief aim of the private secondary schools is to get students ready for college; its subordinate aim is to fit them for life. In the public high school the chief aim is to fit students for life and preparation for college is subordinate."[11]

Most public schools were Protestant-minded, and many used textbooks that were anti-Catholic, reflecting the nativism of the times. The response of the U.S. Catholic bishops was to found parochial schools where Catholic values could be taught. Despite its cost, a parochial school system was designed by the bishops at three plenary councils of Baltimore (1852, 1866, 1884). The last council was headed by Cardinal James Gibbons, bishop of Baltimore, whose strong influence secured widespread financial support for the Catholic schools.

---

[9] The first private school in America, the Collegiate School of New York, was founded by the Dutch Reformed Church in 1638, three years after the founding of the first public school, the Boston Latin School.

[10] See "Private Schooling," *E.R.R.,* 1967 Vol. II, pp. 637-656.

[11] Quoted by Theodore R. Sizer, *Secondary Schools at the Turn of the Century* (1964), p. 34.

Private schools other than Catholic also flourished, partly because of the shortcomings of public schools, which were meagerly supported in many communities. Most of the private schools were in the East, the recognized cultural center of the nation. Increasingly, the newly rich in the West began sending their sons and daughters to eastern finishing schools and prep schools. In a period of heavy foreign immigration, the private school helped older American families to maintain a sense of superiority. President Charles W. Eliot of Harvard observed in 1894 that "the increased heterogeneity of the population" discouraged many parents from putting their children in the melting-pot public schools. Use of the private schools as a "class separator" led to criticism of them after World War I as "undemocratic" and widened the breach between public and private education.

Hard times during the depression of the 1930s played havoc with efforts by private schools to maintain their position. The dozen years after the stock market crash in 1929, a headmaster of Lawrenceville School in New Jersey wrote, "do not constitute . . . the most edifying chapter in the history of these institutions." Schools bid against each other for students and admitted some whose chief qualification was that their parents could pay the tuition. "The whole episode was bad for standards and did the reputation of the private schools no good."[12] With the rising demand for higher education after World War II, private schools tightened their admissions standards and raised tuitions. But while many prospered in one sense, they also faced new challenges in an era of great social change.

Effect of the 1954 Desegregation Decision

A quarter-century ago, on May 17, 1954, the Supreme Court overturned the prevailing "separate but equal" doctrine in public education.[13] The decision set off a revolution in education that has yet to run its course. Although the court's ruling applied to public school systems, private schools also felt the effect.[14]

Integration stimulated new interest in private education among white families, and some black families who shied away from sending their children to public schools that were caught in the cross fire of conflict over desegregation. The growing intensity of the race struggle, marked by rioting in dozens of cities, strengthened the resolve of many parents to keep their children out of public schools where they might encounter abuse from hostile classmates.

---

[12] Allan V. Heely, *Why the Private School?* (1951), pp. 63-64.

[13] For background, see "Educational Equality," *E.R.R.*, 1973 Vol. II, pp. 645-664, and "Desegregation After 20 Years," *E.R.R.*, 1974 Vol. I, pp. 323-342.

[14] *Brown v. Board of Education*, 347 U.S. 483 (1954).

Even before the racial situation reached such a critical point, many city school systems were disturbed by pressures, often from opposing groups of parents, for or against measures used to carry out desegregation. A series of court rulings in the 1960s, ordering drastic steps to modify overt segregation in many of the nation's public schools, was followed by reports of a sharp increase in private school enrollment. Judges mandated busing of children from poor neighborhoods to below-capacity schools in upper-middle-class neighborhoods, more mixing of white and black teachers in city schools, and abandonment in some cases of the track system or ability grouping.

Parents of upper-track students became concerned that the learning pace of their children would slacken as the result of an influx of poor students. Some also feared the effects of their children's association with students from lower-class neighborhoods where crime and delinquency were endemic. Frequent conflicts between school officials and federal agencies, and rumors that good teachers were leaving city school systems further contributed to parental anxiety over the quality of public education.

Rise of Segregated Academies in the South

In a special category of private schools are those that were established purposely to circumvent integrated public schools. More than 200 such schools, some supported by public funds, appeared chiefly in Alabama, Louisiana, Mississippi, South Carolina and Virginia. The generally slow progress of public school desegregation in the South held down the number of these schools. But a federal court ruling in 1966 ordering the immediate desegregation of all public school grades[15] gave new impetus to the establishment of private academies.

Public aid of various kinds for private schools restricted to white children was common in many southern states. But one by one courts ruled out the scholarships, tuition grants, tax credits for donations to new schools and other measures of this kind adopted by legislatures to aid education institutions in circumventing desegregation. In general, the principle the courts followed was that diversion of tax funds to a private school places that school under the same constitutional strictures that apply to a public school.

The Supreme Court struck a major blow at the private school device to evade integration of public schools when in 1964 it ordered the reopening of public schools in Prince Edward County, Va. At the time, the county's public schools had been

---

[15] *United States v. Jefferson County Board of Education*, Civil No. 233345, Fifth Circuit, Dec. 29, 1966.

closed for five years, during which private schools were operated for white children aided by tuition grants. The court held that the black children of the county were being denied equal protection of the law because they were treated differently from children in other counties who had access to public schools.[16]

The anti-desegregation campaign in the South raised and partially clarified several legal questions pertaining to the operation of private schools in general. A federal court ruled in 1965 that segregation in a private school was unconstitutional if the school was "predominantly maintained" by the state.[17] This ruling accorded with a provision of the Civil Rights Act of 1964 which defines a public school as one "operated wholly or predominantly from and through the use of governmental funds."

In August 1966 another federal court broadened the application of the desegregation rule, holding that "any amount of state support to help found segregated schools or to help maintain such schools is sufficient to give standing to Negro school children." The court said state grants that encourage the founding of "quasi-public" segregated schools hurt black pupils by draining away support from the public schools which they had to attend.[18]

Lawsuits brought by civil rights groups led the federal courts to forbid all forms of public assistance to schools that practice racial discrimination. In 1970, the U.S. District Court for the District of Columbia ruled in *Green v. Connally* that racially discriminatory schools in Mississippi were not entitled to tax exemptions. The decision was later upheld by the Supreme Court. In 1975 the IRS provided its first set of guidelines for schools, including religious schools, that wished to retain their exempt status. It required that schools put a non-discrimination clause in their catalogues, and annually advertise in print and broadcast media that they did not discriminate in admissions. When these guidelines did not appear sufficiently effective, the agency proposed new ones and set off the present controversy. Despite the recalcitrance of some schools, integration appears to be moving forward in private education.

Independent Schools' Minority Admissions

Today middle-class black families may be the greatest seekers of private education for their children. Some experts say as many as 40 percent of these families opt for private education, proportionally more than white families in comparable economic circumstances. This is true, authorities say, because

---

[16] *Griffin v. County School Board of Prince Edward County,* 377 U.S. 218 (1964).

[17] *Griffin v. State Board of Education,* 239 F. Supp. 560 (E.D. Va. 1966).

[18] *Poindexter v. Louisiana Financial Assistance Commission,* 258 F. Supp. 158 (E.D. La. 1966).

black families have fewer opportunities than white families to find housing in neighborhoods with "good" public schools.

Many of the barriers to admission of qualified blacks to independent schools fell in the wake of the civil rights movements. In many cases, of course, such barriers never existed. *The Negro Handbook 1966* listed 300 private preparatory schools in 43 states that admitted black students as a matter of policy. The National Association of Independent Schools canvassed its membership the same year and came up with a different set of figures. It found that nine out of ten of the 740 schools responding had open-door policies and that six out of ten had black students enrolled. In all, black students constituted 3.2 percent of the students at the 462 schools at which blacks were enrolled. As of June 1978, black students accounted for 4.5 percent of the total.

The NAIS traditionally has encouraged its member schools to seek black students rather than rest on a passive non-discrimination policy. In 1964, the association advised its members: "There is a special burden on independent schools located in parts of the country which are relatively free from the crisis atmosphere to take leadership in the whole matter of desegregation."[19] From a practical standpoint, the association declared, any institution that wants black students must ask them to attend. "If it has none, it is fair to say that it simply does not want them."

Non-Catholic Blacks in Parochial Schools

There is no way of knowing how many parents have sought out parochial schools as an escape from integrated public schools. The U.S. Civil Rights Commission concluded in 1967 that "private and parochial school enrollment . . . is an important factor in the increasing concentration of Negroes in the city school systems."[20] By the mid-1960s, one out of every seven school children in the United States attended parochial schools. Studies at the time showed that in Boston and St. Louis two-fifths, and in Philadelphia three-fifths, of all white elementary pupils were in non-public (mainly parochial) schools.

Catholic family preference for religious education and the relatively few black Catholics kept most parochial school systems predominantly white. Until the late 1960s, the proportion of white children attending parochial school was larger in cities than in the suburbs, suggesting that city parents may have favored parochial schools as a means of avoiding what many regarded as the "unsettled" conditions in public schools.

---

[19] David Mallery, *Negro Students in Independent Schools* (National Association of Independent Schools publication, December 1963), p. 6.

[20] See U.S. Commission on Civil Rights, *Racial Isolation in the Public Schools,* 1967.

However, black enrollment in the nation's nearly 9,000 parochial schools has steadily increased in recent years. This is the result of demographic changes in neighborhoods as well as the belief on the part of many non-Catholic black parents that parochial schools offer a better education than city public schools. According to the Rev. Patrick Farrell, education director of the U.S. Catholic Conference, as many as 70 percent of the students in some schools come from non-Catholic families. The influx, Father Farrell said, has caused Catholic authorities to reexamine their mission. "We discovered that our real strength was our relationship with the community, and that we offered parents the kind of education that they wanted for their children."[21]

While many Catholic educators view the resurgence of their schools as a hopeful sign, they also see a number of difficulties ahead. The main problem is financial. Most Catholic schools get the bulk of their support from the parishes they serve. But with the migration of Catholic families from the cities to the suburbs, Church membership in urban areas has fallen off and so has support for schools in urban parishes. Officials say that tuition alone isn't enough to meet the cost of schooling. Catholic leaders add that increased federal aid is needed in the form of tuition credits or direct payments to the schools if they are to fulfill their new mission of educating urban minority children.

Changing Role of Private Schools

PARENTS who still think of private schools as havens where their children will be sheltered from the turmoil enveloping public schools may be disappointed. Perhaps the most significant recent development in private education is its growing involvement with the world beyond the campus. Often the more aristocratic and exclusive a school's reputation, the more likely it is to be cultivating a more democratic image. This is most strikingly evidenced in the change in admissions policies. Private school students are still a rather select group, but a trend toward heterogeneity in the student body is becoming more and more evident.

Current trends toward enlargement and democratization could reshape the traditional role of the independent school in American education. While mass education has been, and continues to be, the function of public and parochial schools, the

---

[21] Quoted in *U.S. News & World Report,* March 20, 1978.

purpose of the independents has been mainly to give some of the ablest students a high-quality preparation for college. The college admission record of graduates of private schools is, in fact, one of their principal attractions. Of the 825 schools currently represented by the NAIS, two-thirds of the institutions reported that all of their 1977 graduates entered college.

But public schools also have been turning out bright and well-prepared candidates for college, and it is obvious that even in the most demanding colleges the majority of the students are products of the public education systems. However, if parents of abler students come increasingly to favor private schooling for their children, and if the availability of scholarships for bright students from poor families continues to increase, it is conceivable that the distinctions between the educational functions of public and private schools will become sharper than ever.

Despite higher tuitions and inflationary pressures on family spending power, enrollment at 622 independent schools reporting in a 1978 NAIS survey climbed by 1.2 percent. This increase is significant in light of the declining pool of school-age children which has already forced the closing or consolidation of many public schools around the country. Citing reasons for growth in independent school enrollment, NAIS President John C. Esty said: "Families are past caring about educational theories and experimentation. They ask only their children be exposed to decent adults, unharried by excessive numbers and extravagant demands, who can help them individually. That seems to me to be the special attraction of the independent school."[22]

The gradual loss to public school systems of their best students, from poor and rich families alike, could have a significant effect on the direction of public education. It could bring about a de-emphasis of honors courses for the gifted, more attention to "practical" subjects for those not going to college, and added stress on new compensatory programs for the culturally deprived and slow learner. While private schools continue to progress, some educators feel, public schools could easily devolve into "academic hospitals."

Financing Tuition Payments With Vouchers

With Congress' rejection of a tuition tax credit plan last year,[23] advocates of government assistance to families with children in private schools began looking for alternatives. One such approach is now emerging in California. It is a campaign aimed

---

[22] Speaking at NAIS convention, Washington, D.C., March 2, 1979.

[23] A comprehensive tuition tax credit bill was introduced in the Senate last year by Sens. Robert Packwood, R-Ore., and Daniel Patrick Moynihan, D-N.Y. The bill, which ultimately was defeated in the House, would have given parents of children in private schools, including private colleges, a $500 income tax credit. See "College Tuition Costs," *E.R.R.*, 1978 Vol. I, pp. 141-159.

at giving public subsidies to parents to be used to send their children to whatever schools the family chooses — including private and religious schools. This idea, during 20 years of discussion, has come to be known as "voucher education"; as envisioned, the state gives the parents a voucher which entitles them to receive payment for most of the cost of educating their children at a school of their choosing.

The most recent version of this idea, drafted by two law professors at the University of California at Berkeley, John Coons and Stephen Sugarman, would give California parents the first voucher system in practice in the country. Proponents of the plan say that it would restore "family control" to educational decision-making at the elementary and secondary school levels.

The proposal is sure to be hotly contested by the education establishment in California. Sharon Bowman, speaking for the California Teachers Association, said: "We'll put everything we have . . . into defeating the measure."[24] She predicted that the state's professional associations of school boards and school administrators would take a similar stand. But Bowman already concedes that in her opinion the combined forces of California teachers and administrators will not be able to keep the required number of Californians (500,000) from signing petitions to put the voucher proposal on the ballot in the June 1980 primary election.

The proposal emerged from a book in which Coons and Sugarman argued: "The interests of children are best served in a decentralized polity giving maximum scope to free, chosen, communal relationships that are generally organized on a small scale. . . . This suggests to us the strengthening of the family's role in education and the growth of a teaching fraternity which is related to the family as professional to client rather than as master to servant."[25] The main provisions of the Coons-Sugarman Plan:

1. Provide parents a basic voucher worth 90 percent of the current cost of education per child in the public schools.

2. Allow private schools to receive vouchers, provided they meet certain requirements, such as agreeing to admit students without regard to race, religion, or academic ability. (A school with more applicants than spaces would have to conduct a lottery.)

3. Provide supplementary vouchers which parents could purchase. The basic voucher would cost them nothing. The state legislature would set varying prices for those supplementary

---

[24] Quoted in *Family Protection Report* (a Washington-based newsletter), March 1979.

[25] John Coons and Stephen Sugarman, *Education by Choice: The Case for Family Control* (1978), p. 20.

How Voucher System Works

(1)

PROPERTY TAX
provides funds for
education

(2)

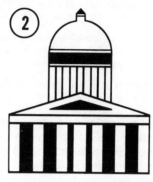

STATE TREASURY
gives tuition vouchers to
families

(3)

FAMILIES
use vouchers to pay
tuition at qualified
schools of their choice

(4)

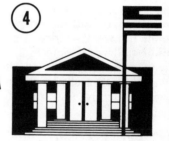

SCHOOLS
return used vouchers to
state treasury

(5)

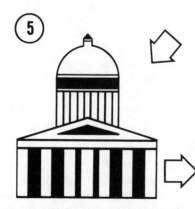

STATE TREASURY   reimburses   **SCHOOLS**

vouchers, depending on family wealth and number of children, so
that richer parents would pay more, poorer parents less.

4. Prohibit participating private schools from charging parents
more than the value of the basic and supplementary vouchers.

5. Allow participating private schools to hire teachers who do
not meet state certification requirements to teach moral values,
philosophy and religion.

6. Put a ceiling on all public expenditures for elementary and
secondary education.

Exactly how the voucher system would work in California has
not been spelled out in the proposed ballot initiative for several
reasons, its sponsors said. For one, it would make the ballot too
long. Also, they said, laws and regulations written by the state
legislature could be tailored to changing educational needs,
whereas a detailed constitutional provision would be inflexible.

Ralph Flynn, executive secretary of the California Teachers
Association, said that any plan based on the Coons-Sugarman
proposals would cost too much, would promote greater racial
segregation, and would lead to an "Oklahoma land rush" of
profit-hungry entrepreneurs eager to tap into a new bonanza of
public funds. "The idea of a private enterprise totally funded by
public dollars is something that never was and never will be,"
Flynn said. He predicted that new private schools founded to
take advantage of the program would band together to form a
powerful lobby and milk the state for further benefits to
themselves.[26]

Proponents see the initiative in a different light. Vouchers,
they say, would make better education available to every
California family. Instead of having to send their children to the
public school in their neighborhood, parents would be able to
choose from any number of other schools. In addition, supporters contend, as more and more families send their children to
private institutions under the voucher system, educators would
be forced to improve the quality of public schools. Robert Mar-
lowe of the Washington-based Council for Educational Freedom
in America called the California initiative drive "a step in the
right direction."

Discarding the Image of Exclusive Wealth

Perhaps the most significant trend in private schools in recent
years is their effort to erase the impression that they are the
exclusive preserves of the wealthy. The increased recruitment of
minority students along with the admission of girls to formerly
all-male enclaves have changed the educational and social

---

[26] Quoted in *Family Protection Report.*

environment on many campuses. Student bodies have become more representative of the society as a whole.

"In an egalitarian 20th century, private schools suffer from a bad conscience," Laurence McMillin wrote over a decade ago.[27] Educators say that is no longer the case, that private schools are committed to serving a broader social purpose than they have in the past. They point to aggressive programs in gaining minority faculty members and students as proof, on one level at least, that they are rapidly catching up with the times. A Better Chance (ABC), a student recruitment program sponsored by the NAIS since 1963, has placed more than 5,000 minority pupils in private schools, some 3,100 of whom have graduated and gone on to college. The association reported in 1968 its member schools provided $16.5 million in financial aid to "needy" students; in 1978 they provided $50.5 million, with approximately one-third going to minority students.

The chief value of independent schools usually cited is that they are free to try new ways of teaching and thus serve as proving grounds for innovations in all schools. The zest for experimentation is indeed riding high, with schools across the country introducing programs directed toward bringing students into closer touch with the world beyond the campus. But administrators of private schools say "the outside world," particularly the federal government, may present the greatest challenge to their continued survival. Theodore Sizer, headmaster of Phillips Academy, has said:

> If we want to democratize the non-public school sector, to give it the sustained support necessary for rigorous standards, and to extend the freedom of choice to students and families below the college level, we need substantial public support. At the same time, such public support might induce, through regulation, a new homegeneity, eliminating ironically any virtue to the choices available. We are caught in a dilemma, and the wisdom we show in resolving this dilemma will be the measure of how we survive.[28]

The relationship of private institutions with the public sector has long been a source of social conflict. Private schools, in their effort to become more pluralistic, must balance the requirements accompanying federal assistance with the tradition of academic freedom. How well they do so may determine whether or not they continue to be distinct, independent educational institutions.

---

[27] Laurence McMillin, "Big Education: Can Independent Schools Survive?" *The Independent School Bulletin,* February 1967, p. 10.

[28] Speaking in Andover, Mass., June 4, 1978.

Selected Bibliography

Books

Eidenberg, Eugene and Roy D. Morey, *An Act of Congress: The Legislative Process and the Making of Education Policy*, Norton, 1969.

Kraushaar, Otto F., *Private Schools: From the Puritans to the Present*, Phi Delta Kappa Press, 1976.

Lightfoot, Sarah L., *Worlds Apart: Relationships Between Families and Schools*, Basic Books, 1978.

McMillan, William J., *Private School Management*, Peters Press, 1977.

Metz, Mary Haywood, *Classroom and Corridors: The Crisis of Authority in Desegregated Secondary Schools*, University of California Press, 1978.

Nevin, David and Robert E. Bills, *The Schools That Fear Built: Segregationist Academies in the South*, Acropolis Books, 1976.

Orfield, Gary, *The Reconstruction of Southern Education*, Wiley-Interscience, 1969.

Articles

Dandridge, William L., "Recruiting Minority Teachers for Independent Schools," *Independent School*, December 1978.

Education Daily, selected issues.

"Feeling Threatened by the IRS: Racial Guidelines for Private Schools," *Time*, Dec. 18, 1978.

Hechinger, Fred M., "Schoolyard Blues,: The Decline of Public Education," *Saturday Review*, Jan. 20, 1978.

"HEW and Private Schools," *America*, May 20, 1978.

Independent School, selected issues.

Kilpatrick, James J., "Tuition Grants and Trojan Horses," *Nation's Business*, October 1978.

Moynihan, Daniel P., "Government and the Ruin of Private Education: Tuition Tax Credits," *Harper's*, April 1978.

Powell, Arthur, "Three Emerging Educational Issues," *Independent School*, February 1979.

"Seven Cardinal Principles Revisited," *Today's Education*, September 1976.

Silber, John R., "Need for Elite Education," *Harper's*, June 1977.

"Vast Changes Ahead for U.S. Schools," *U.S. News & World Report*, Feb. 14, 1977.

Reports and Studies

College Entrance Examination Board, "Middle-Income Students: A New Target for Federal Aid?" June 1978.

Editorial Research Reports, "Private Schooling," 1967 Vol. II, p. 637; "Coeducation: New Growth," 1969 Vol. I, p. 329; "Educational Equality," 1973 Vol. II, p. 645.

Espenshade, Thomas J., "The Value and Cost of Children," Population Reference Bureau, April 1977.

U.S. Senate, "Description of Bills Relating to Tuition Credits and Deductions Listed for Hearing by the Subcommittee on Taxation and Debt Management of the Committee on Finance," Jan. 17, 1978.

COMPETENCY TESTS

by

Marc Leepson

**Aug. 18
1 9 7 8**

Editors Note: In August 1981, the Education Commission of the States reported competency testing was being conducted in 36 states, two more than when this report was first published in August 1978.

COMPETENCY TESTS

PARENTS, EDUCATORS and employers have voiced new concerns about the quality of American education in the last several years. The worry is that elementary and secondary schools are turning out increasing numbers of high school graduates who are weak in the basic skills of reading, writing and arithmetic. Declining test scores on national and state examinations since the mid-1960s also have prompted questions about the nation's educational system. Last year, a Gallup Poll indicated that many American adults have serious doubts about the quality of American education *(see box, p. 161)*. Parents nationwide have complained that while education costs are rising, the quality of education is sinking.[1] "Generally, we seem to have seen a nationwide academic achievement decline," author Frank E. Armbruster wrote last year after studying scores on academic achievement tests given to all grades in most states.[2]

One reaction to this perceived decline has been the movement toward returning to traditional methods of teaching.[3] And one off-shoot of the trend back to basics is the adoption by many states of standardized, mandatory minimal competency tests, especially as requirements for high school graduation. Edward B. Fiske Jr., education editor of *The New York Times,* wrote April 19 that the setting of minimal academic standards in the form of competency tests is "perhaps the most powerful movement in American public education."

Since 1975, 34 states have established programs that require some form of minimal competency testing, according to the Denver-based Education Commission of the States, a non-profit organization that promotes cooperation among state and federal government leaders ine ducation *(see table, p. 163)*. The movement by state legislatures and boards of education to establish minimal competency tests in elementary and secondary schools has been called "one of the most explosive issues on the education scene today" by the Education Commission's research and information director, Russell B. Vlaanderen.[4]

---

[1] The National Center for Education Statistics estimates that public and private elementary and secondary schools spent some $91 billion in 1977-78.

[2] Frank E. Armbruster, *Our Children's Crippled Future* (1977), p. 176.

[3] See "Education's Return to Basics," *E.R.R.,* 1975 Vol. II, p. 667.

[4] Writing in the introduction to "Update VII: Minimal Competency Testing," prepared by Chris Pipho, Education Commission of the States, Nov. 15, 1977.

The minimal competency movement has generated controversy. There is disagreement in the education community about the need for the tests and about their effect on students and teachers. In general, the pressure for competency tests has come from outside the education establishment — from parents, business leaders, military recruiters and even college admission officials. These groups have expressed widespread dissatisfaction with the educational performance of American public schools. They are concerned with the numbers of high school graduates who lack basic skills.

Disagreement About Necessity of Tests

Proponents of minimal competency tests regard them as a "guarantee" that high school graduates possess minimal reading, writing and mathematical skills. Opponents of competency-based education generally are teachers and officials of teachers' unions. They resent the implication that the schools failed to educate students properly. They have expressed concerns about the validity and reliability of competency tests, and the fact that the tests measure only a fraction of what students learn in school.

The evidence that high school graduates are lacking basic skills has come from many sources. Colleges nationwide have been forced to set up remedial reading programs for entering freshmen. Last fall, for example, some 1,700 students in the 7,100-member freshman class at Ohio State University were required to take remedial English; some 2,000 had to take remedial math. Military recruiters have experienced difficulties finding young men who read well enough to perform the more demanding military jobs. Since 1977, the Navy has required many of its recruits to enroll in six-week remedial courses aimed at raising reading abilities to the sixth-grade level.

The National Assessment of Education Progress (NAEP), which is funded by the U.S. Department of Health, Education and Welfare, estimates that 13 percent of the nation's 17-year-old high school students are functionally illiterate. That is — according to the NAEP definition of the term — they are not "able to perform tasks necessary to function in American society, such as reading newspapers, instructions and even drivers' license tests." Those figures, released early in 1977, were compiled in a study called the "Right to Read Report" comparing functional reading performances of more than 4,200 17-year-old students in 1971, 1974 and 1975. The study found that 21 percent of the 17-year-old students from urban areas, 42 percent of the black students nationwide and 20 percent of the students from southeastern states were functionally illiterate.

Adults Grade Schools

A Gallup Poll released in September 1977 indicated that more adult Americans than ever before are more inclined to give poor marks to the nation's public schools. To measure the quality of public school education in their own communities, some 1,500 adults were asked the following question:

"Students are often given the grades A, B, C, D, and FAIL to denote the quality of their work. Suppose the public schools themselves, in this community, were graded in the same way. What grade would you give the public schools here — A, B, C, D, or FAIL?"

Ratings Given the Public Schools	1977	National Totals 1976	1975	1974
A Rating	11%	13%	13%	18%
B Rating	26	29	30	30
C Rating	28	28	28	21
D Rating	11	10	9	6
Fail	5	6	7	5
Don't know/ No answer	19	14	13	20

Several "education malpractice" lawsuits have been brought against school districts — another indication of unhappiness with American public education. The first such lawsuit was filed by a high school graduate of the San Francisco public school system in 1972. He sought to have a California court attribute his inability to read to negligence by education authorities. That $1 million suit was dismissed. But there are other similar cases pending across the country, including a $5 million suit against the Copiague, N.Y., school district brought by the parents of a high school graduate who, they say, is barely literate and cannot get a job.

Differences in State Testing Programs

One of the earliest programs in the nation requiring passage of a minimal competency test as a requirement for high school graduation was drawn up in Denver, Colo., in 1958. A public opinion survey of business and industrial employers in the Denver area had indicated that many high school graduates lacked competence in basic skills. Many business leaders and parents were questioning the validity of a high school diploma. The Denver Proficiency and Review Program, designed to assure that every high school graduate possesses minimum competency in arithmetic, spelling, grammar and reading comprehension, went into effect in 1960. Since then, any senior who does not pass all four tests receives no diploma. Instead, a certificate of attendance is given.

The Denver tests are given twice a year, starting in the ninth grade, based on material appropriate for the sixth grade. A student who fails one or more tests receives extra instruction and is then tested again. The idea behind the Denver program is to get as many students as possible to pass the tests before they reach the 12th grade. Since the testing began, the failure rate for seniors has been about 1.5 percent. Denver school officials say they are happy with the program. "In general, we are pleased with the results of this approach," Barry B. Beal, supervisor of development and evaluation for Denver public schools, told a House subcommittee last year. "We are now looking into the possibility of testing children as early as the end of the third and sixth grades with the idea being to pick up weaknesses even sooner than we do now."[5]

Colorado law lets each local school district draw up its own tests and standards. In several other states *(see listing)*, the legislatures or boards of education have mandated the use of statewide minimal competency tests for high school graduation and grade promotion. Oregon was the first to legislate statewide proficiency testing. In 1972, the state Board of Education ordered that reading, writing and computation tests be passed as a high school graduation requirement beginning this year.

Local districts in Oregon have been given leeway in developing their own standards, including optional use of minimal competency tests for grade-level assessment. "We in Oregon feel the program can work," Superintendent of Public Instruction Verne A. Duncan said last year. "And although it has placed additional burdens on local school districts, we feel the end result will be better education for Oregon's students and a better way to make sure that every child will have the skills necessary to cope in our complex society."[6]

Last fall, Florida became the first state to put into effect a competency-based system. The state legislature passed a law in 1976 prescribing that students pass statewide functional literacy and mathematics tests in order to graduate from high school. In addition, each grade has a series of basic skill tests to determine whether or not a student is promoted. Of the 100,000 Florida 11th graders who took the first tests last fall, 36 percent failed the math and 8 percent failed the reading and writing sections. Those who failed must take the test again and pass it in order to graduate. In some districts the failure rate was very high. About 90 percent of the students at Jean Ribault High School in Jacksonville failed the math tests. Some 77 percent of the black

---

[5] Testifying before the House Subcommittee on Elementary, Secondary and Vocational Education of the Education and Labor Committee, Sept. 14, 1977.

[6] Testifying before the House Subcommittee on Elementary, Secondary and Vocational Education of the Education and Labor Committee, May 11, 1977.

Minimal Competency Testing
State-by-State Summary

State	Action Taken By	Type
Ala.	Board of Education	Basic skills
Ariz.	Dept. of Education	Reading, writing, computation
Calif.	Legislature	Reading, writing, computation (effective 1980)
Colo.	Legislature	Local district option
Del.	Board of Education	Reading, writing, math
Fla.	Legislature	Basic skills; functional literacy
Idaho*	Board of Education	Reading, writing, math, spelling
Ky.	Board of Education	Reading, writing, math
Md.	Legislature	Reading
Nev.	Legislature	Reading, writing, math
N.Y.	Board of Regents	Reading, math, civics, citizenship, practical science, drug education, writing health,
N.C.	Legislature	To be determined (effective 1979)
Ore.*	Board of Education	Reading, writing, computation
Tenn.	Board of Education	Reading, math, grammar, spelling (effective 1982)
Utah*	Board of Education	Reading, writing, speaking, listening, math, democratic governance, consumerism, problem solving (effective 1980)
Vt.	Board of Education	Reading, writing, speaking, listening, math
Va.	Legislature	Statewide test (effective 1981)
Wyo.*	Board of Education	Reading, writing, computation (effective date to be determined)

Tests for Remediation and/or Grade Promotion

Arizona, California, Florida, Indiana, Maryland, New Jersey, Tennessee

Laws or Rules on Competency Tests Awaiting Implemention

Georgia, Kansas, Maine, Oklahoma

Competency Programs not Involving Graduation or Grade Promotion

Louisiana, Massachusetts, Michigan, Missouri, Nebraska, New Hampshire, New Mexico,** Rhode Island, Washington

*Local districts establish standards
**Proficiency endorsement on high school diploma if test is passed

Source: Education Commission of the States, as of July 10, 1978

11th graders in Dade County (Miami) failed the tests, leading to charges by groups including the National Association for the Advancement of Colored People that the exams were culturally biased and emphasized white middle-class skills and values.

Criticism of Florida's Statewide Exams

Teacher representatives also have challenged the Florida tests. "I'm not quarreling with such a test per se, but with the misuse of the test," said Yvonne Burkholtz of the Florida Education Associations United, a statewide union of some 35,000 teachers. "We have serious reservations about the speed with which it was implemented, without time for the 11th graders to get remedial instruction. The state acted hastily, and did not think through all the components."[7] Florida education officials maintain that the tests are fair and that the program is proceeding smoothly. The tests "are the most popular thing to hit the state in years," Thomas Fisher, the state's director of student assessment, said recently.[8]

The National Education Association, the nation's largest teacher's organization with some 1.8 million members, sponsored a study of the Florida program. The NEA study, which was co-sponsored by its Florida affiliate, The Florida Teaching Profession-NEA, was conducted by three research professors and two classroom teachers. While praising the purpose of the program, the study group's report characterized it as "seriously faulty." The report criticized the use of statewide standards, maintaining that local school boards should set their own competency-test policies.

It said that competency test results reflect more than the quality of education students receive in school. It said the high failure rate in some areas was caused by "the eroding education environment outside the school."[9] The report suggested that competency tests should be used to identify students who need help rather than withhold a high school diploma or grade promotion. Terry Herndon, executive director of the NEA, said the study showed "the tyranny of impersonalized, standardized testing with specifications set at some kind of 'norm' that ignores the individual child and the judgment of teachers."[10]

In some states there has been little movement to institute statewide minimal competency tests. One such state is Wisconsin, which is generally recognized as having an effective public school system. There are statewide testing programs mandated by law in Wisconsin, but they are not related to graduation

---

[7] Quoted in the *Los Angeles Times,* May 12, 1978.
[8] Quoted in *The Wall Street Journal,* May 9, 1978.
[9] National Education Association and The Florida Teaching Profession-NEA, "The Florida Accountability Program, etc.," July 1978, p. 14.
[10] Quoted in *The New York Times,* July 4, 1978.

requirements. Wisconsin's Department of Public Instruction is headed by the elected state superintendent of public instruction, Barbara Thompson. In January, she named a task force of 29 persons — school administrators, representatives of teachers unions and others — to study the situation. After six months, the group recommended not to set up statewide minimal competency tests and instead leave the decision with local districts.

"We're aware that we are bucking the national trend," Darwin Kaufman, evaluation supervisor of the Department of Public Instruction, told Editorial Research Reports. "And I think we keep wondering about whether somebody — a single legislator or some parent group — will provide the motivation" that will induce the legislature to set up a program. "In local districts there is an increasing amount of interest, which we've measured only by the number of calls we get to talk to teachers about competency-based education. But I've found that interest by a local district and actually getting involved in it presents quite a gap."

Push for National Competency Standards

The minimal competency movement led last year to committee hearings in both the U.S. House and Senate to determine whether national standards in reading, writing and mathematics should be established. Rep. Ronald M. Mottl, D-Ohio, drafted a bill last year to require every state to give all students proficiency tests in reading, writing and math in order to qualify for federal education money. If standards developed by a national commission were not met, a student could not graduate from high school anywhere in the United States.

Mottl's measure was greeted by a roar of disapproval from educators who charged that it trod on the traditional prerogatives of states to run their educational systems without federal interference. His legislation did not emerge from the congressional committee it was assigned. Mottl said last year that he introduced the bill because of his belief that states and local school districts have been lax in devising methods of testing minimal competency. "If this does one thing, it will prod local districts into action," Mottl said. "I don't mind being the 'heavy.' We need to set national standards and give them a gauge."[11]

The federal government has taken some action on competency-based education. Mary F. Berry, assistant secretary for education in HEW, last year created the Task Force on Basic Skills and Quality Education to review the evidence concerning standards of quality in the nation's schools. The task force,

---

[11] Quoted in *Congressional Quarterly Weekly Report,* Oct. 15, 1977, p. 2202.

which included nationally known education researchers, recommended against setting up national or statewide minimal competency tests. The institution of standardized minimal standards, the group reported, "is basically unworkable, exceeds the present measurement arts of the teaching profession and will create more social problems than it can conceivably solve."[12] It recommended standardized tests for lower grades but cautioned that they be used "with care, and with increased public...understanding of the diagnostic and therapeutic use (and limitations) of tests...." The report said that, properly administered, "minimum competency testing can be a positive educational development."

HEW Secretary Joseph A. Califano Jr. and President Carter both favor the use of competency tests, but only in certain situations. "Basic competency tests, used skillfully and sensitively, are useful and necessary," Califano told the annual meeting of the College Entrance Examination Board last year. "Basic competency testing will be acceptable and effective only if we stress, along with its benefits, the critical limitations and dangers of testing." Califano said the limitations included imprecise methods of scoring and possible cultural bias in the questions. He also warned that the tests are not a true reflection of what children learn in school and cautioned that some teachers tend to gear their teaching toward what will be tested. Califano has said that Carter believes testing is a state matter.

HEW has established an office to assess competency tests and is conducting research to determine the extent of the federal role, if any. Pending congressional legislation would allow federal funds to be used to train teachers and administrators in giving competency tests and in publicizing their benefits. That legislation, part of the 1978 amendments to the 1965 Elementary and Secondary Education Act Amendments, has been passed by the House and awaits Senate action.

Modern Educational Testing

WHILE COMPETENCY tests have been used on a statewide basis only in the last three years, modern educational testing dates from around the turn of the century. Educators at that time were interested in the idea that mental capacity could be measured mathematically. A French psychologist, Alfred Binet, was commissioned by the French minister of public in-

---

[12] National Academy of Education, "Improving Educational Achievement: Report of the National Academy Education Commission on Testing and Basic Skills," 1978, p. iv.

struction to create an effective measuring device. Binet and an assistant, Theodore Simon, developed a series of graded tests to determine the ability of children to meet the demands of primary education. Among the areas of knowledge tested were whether a child knew left from right, could follow simple directions and recall a series of numbers.

The Binet test, first published in 1905 and revised in 1908 and 1911, attracted worldwide attention and launched a flurry of experimentation. The Binet tests were first applied in the United States by Lewis Terman of Stanford University and Henry Goddard of the Vineland Training School in New Jersey. American versions of the Binet-Simon test appeared in 1916.

The U.S. armed forces began testing military personnel for mental ability during World War I. A group of psychologists, headed by Edward L. Thorndike, produced the famous Army Alpha, which was used to classify more than a million draftees by intelligence levels. The Army Alpha was a verbal test designed to be taken only by those with at least a sixth-grade education. Another test was used for illiterates and draftees who spoke only a foreign language. A personality test was developed for identification and study of suspected neurotics among draftees, and some progress was made in working out aptitude tests to identify suitable candidates for specific kinds of military duty.

After World War I, the Army tests were made available for civilian use. Thousands of high school and college students took the Army Alpha, and psychologists and educators set out to develop tests to evaluate nearly every aspect of human ability. Question construction techniques and statistical methods of scoring, first developed for the mental measurement tests, were adapted to tests for evaluating student achievement. Teachers in large numbers discarded the traditional essay-type question and used true-false, multiple-choice or other short-answer type questions.

General Acceptance Since World War II

World War II put a powerful spur to the testing movement. By that time, author Jacques Barzun wrote, "testing by check-mark was established practice everywhere in American life — in the school system, in business, in the professions, in the administration of law and in the work of hospitals and institutions for the mentally deranged."[13] All branches of the armed forces used standardized tests as an aid to classifying and assigning personnel. Cooperation between colleges and universities and the military, beginning in World War II, gave many educational in-

---

[13] Writing in the introduction of Banesh Hoffmann's *Tyranny of Testing* (1962), p. 7.

stitutions their first intensive experience in the development and use of standardized tests.

In 1957, the American education establishment was thrown into a frenzy with the Russian launching of Sputnik I, the first man-made earth satellite. Suddenly, Americans realized they were behind in the space race and something had to be done to catch up. Congress passed laws to provide scholarships and grants to improve math, science and foreign-language instruction. Guidance counseling was stressed as never before; more audio-visual aids were developed for the classroom. Testing programs were vastly increased to try to judge the extent of the problem.

In an attempt to reach more students, many new teaching techniques were instituted during the late 1950s and early 1960s. "We innovated all over the place," wrote John I. Goodlad, dean of the graduate school of education at the University of California, Los Angeles, "with new approaches to curriculum content; with programmed and computerized instruction; with modular scheduling, modular buildings, and acoustically treated walls, ceilings and floors; with nongrading, team teaching, and flexible grouping; with films, film strips, multimedia 'packages,' and television instruction."[14] ˜

Decline of Test Scores in High Schools

In spite of these innovations, the average scores on nationwide and statewide tests — including the Scholastic Aptitude Test, American College Tests, Minnesota Scholastic Aptitude Test, Iowa Tests of Educational Development and Basic Skills and the Comprehensive Tests of Basic Skills — began to decline in the early 1960s. Test scores on the College Entrance Examination Board's Scholastic Aptitude Test, taken by more than one million high school juniors and seniors annually, have fallen steadily since 1963 *(see opposite page)*. The average verbal score on the test, which is given to help forecast how a high school student will perform in college, declined from 478 in 1962-63 to 429 in 1976-77. The average math score dropped from 502 in 1962-63 to 471 in 1976-77.[15] The tests are scored on a scale from 200 to 800.

Scores on tests administered by the American College Testing Program (ACT), based in Iowa City, Iowa, have also fallen during the last 10 years for which data are available. The average composite score of the ACT tests, which are taken by some 900,000 high school students annually in English, math, social studies and natural sciences, has declined from 19.9 in 1969-70 to

---

[14] John I. Goodlad, "An Emphasis on Change," *American Education,* January-February 1975, p. 21.

[15] Scores for 1977-78 are due to be released Sept. 10, 1978.

National Test Scores

School Year	SAT[1] Score Averages		ACT[2] Score Averages
	Verbal	Mathematical	Composite
1962-63	478	502	NA[3]
1963-64	475	498	NA[3]
1964-65	473	496	19.9
1965-66	471	496	20.0
1966-67	467	495	19.4
1967-68	466	494	19.0
1968-69	462	491	19.4
1969-70	460	488	19.9
1970-71	454	487	19.2
1971-72	450	482	19.1
1972-73	443	481	19.2
1973-74	440	478	18.9
1974-75	437	473	18.6
1975-76	429	470	18.3
1976-77	429	471	18.4
1977-78	NA[4]	NA[4]	18.5

[1] Scholastic Aptitude Test. Scale ranges from 200 to 800.
[2] American College Testing Program. Scale ranges from 1 to 36.
[3] Not Available.
[4] Available Sept. 10, 1978

Source: College Entrance Examination Board and the American College Testing Program.

18.5 in 1977-78. The ACT scale ranges from 1 to 36. Since the mid-1960s test scores for high school juniors have declined on the Minnesota Scholastic Aptitude Test; scores in all areas for grades 5 through 12 have declined in the Iowa Tests of Educational Development; national norm data of the Iowa Tests of Basic Skills show drops in language, mathematics and reading; and national norm data on the Comprehensive Tests of Basic Skills show declines in mathematics and reading from grade 5 and language from grades 6 through 10.

Declining scores have been interpreted by many to mean that the quality of American education is slipping. A study conducted by the National Association of Secondary School Principals found that students scored considerably higher SAT scores at schools that stressed academic courses such as mathematics, foreign languages, English and physical science than students at schools that experimented with new approaches in curriculum content. The schools across the country where SAT scores rose, the study found, "took certain initiatives or else maintained some specific 'standards' that they considered important to the success of their college-bound students."[16]

[16] National Association of Secondary School Principals, "Guidelines for Improving SAT Scores," 1978, p. 4.

Competency Tests for Teachers?

Education officials across the country have begun discussing measuring the quality of their public schools through the use of minimal competency tests — not for students, but for teachers. The Virginia legislature adopted a resolution this year calling for a study of the administration of a test of minimal competency for teachers. In New York, the vice chancellor of the State Board of Regents, Willard A. Genrich, said July 28: "It would seem only fair that if we've mandated tests for children, we should have them for teachers as well."

Across the country teachers are certified in several different ways. Most states require that teachers successfully complete certain university courses and have supervisory classroom experience. A few jurisdictions have special tests for teacher licensing.

The results of a test given to first-year classroom teachers recently in Dallas proved to be an embarrassment to the school system. On July 18 the *Dallas Times Herald* reported that more than half of the 535 teachers who took an exam designed to measure the intelligence of individuals 13 years or older failed the test. The test was a brief, two-part examination of verbal and mathematical ability. "According to the testing results," the newspaper reported, "there were 11 classroom teachers . . . who scored 20 or below — or they missed at least 50 of the 60 questions on the test."

The College Entrance Examination Board set up an advisory panel headed by former Secretary of Labor Willard Wirtz in 1975 to look into the test-score decline. The panel's report, issued in August 1977, found no single force or closely related set of forces responsible for the decline. The panel concluded that there have been two stages in the decline — one between 1963 and 1970, and the other since 1970. The first decline was caused by a marked change in students who took the test, the Wirth panel said. Each year between 1963 and 1970, those taking the test "included larger proportions of characteristically lower-scoring groups of students" — who were identified mainly as children of poor or black families and, in the case of math scores, girls. "This pulled the overall average down."[17]

The post-1970 decline, the panel reported, probably has been caused by many factors, including: (1) the movement away from basics and to elective courses, especially in English, (2) "clearly observable evidence of diminished seriousness of purpose and attention to mastery of skills and knowledge in the learning process as it proceeds in the schools, the home, and the society generally," (3) the prevalence of television watching, and (4) an "apparent diminution in young people's learning motivation."

[17] College Entrance Examination Board, "On Further Examination: Report of the Advisory Panel on the Scholastic Aptitude Test Score Decline," 1977, p. 13.

Others have pointed out that the SAT declines cannot be viewed as an indication of the lowering of quality of American education overall, because only a relatively small percentage of high school students take the test and because the tests are designed to aid in college admission screening rather than indicate the quality of American education. But — aside from the declining standardized tests scores — there exist other indications of the declining achievement of American elementary and secondary students.

The National Assessment of Education Progress (NAEP) has conducted numerous studies to measure the benefits of American education. The latest NAEP study, released April 9, 1978, found that less than 40 percent of the nation's 17-year-old students spend as much as five hours a week on homework. Moreover, nearly half of the 17-year-olds surveyed said they watch at least one hour of television on school nights. The nationwide survey, given over a 10-week period in 1976, was based on a questionnaire answered by 10,014 students. The mathematical abilities of the same students were also tested; students who reported doing the most homework and the least amount of television watching scored highest.

Other recent NAEP studies indicated that during the first half of the 1970s American teenagers showed declines in their knowledge of the structure and function of government and lost ground in understanding the political process. In one 1976 survey, only about one-fifth of the 13-year-olds could identify at least one of their congressional representatives. Slightly less than half of the 17-year-olds could do so.

Attempts to Measure Educational Quality

Partly as a reaction to the declining test scores, some states adopted varying systems to define and measure the quality of education in their schools between 1963 and 1974. Accountability laws, designed to measure the adequacy and efficiency of educational programs offered by the public schools, were drafted in a number of states, including Colorado, which passed an Educational Accountability Act in 1971. Some states, such as California, passed laws to determine the competency of teachers. But the movement to set up statewide standards of minimal competency for students did not take hold until a few years ago. "As recently as 1974," Rutgers University law professor Paul L. Tractenberg wrote last year, "there was virtually no evaluation of pupil performance against established statewide standards for ...promotion from grade to grade or high school graduation."[18]

---

[18] Paul L. Tractenberg, "The Legal Implications of Statewide Pupil Performance Standards," a background paper prepared for the Minimal Competency Workshops, sponsored by the Education Commission of the States, September 1977.

Most states required high school graduates to complete certain courses, such as American history, state history, citizenship, civics or patriotism. Statewide standardized tests, like the New York Regents examinations, were used only to identify outstanding students and reward them with graduation honors. A number of states, including Colorado, set up minimal competency standards for local districts. The widespread movement to establish statewide tests began in 1975 when nearly all of the states started studying the implementation of programs involving minimal pupil performance.

Future of Competency Tests

ONE OF THE primary concerns about competency testing programs is what happens to those who complete four years of high school study but fail minimal competency tests. "Imagine going out [looking] for a job with a certificate of attendance instead of a diploma," said James McDermott, a Washington state senator. "It would be like not getting an honorable discharge from the military, regardless of the reasons."[19] McDermott and others have argued that as more states adopt minimal competency standards, more high school seniors will be denied graduation for failing competency tests. This could have serious social and political consequences, adding to teenage unemployment and its attendant problems.

Some states administer high school graduation competency tests to students as early as the ninth grade and set up remediation programs for those who fail. Other states deal differently with the failures. They award special diplomas, certificates of competency, diplomas with an endorsement certifying that the student has or has not met specified competencies or certificates of attendance. "Whatever route is selected," a National Association of Secondary School Principals study found, "will likely draw some complaint because qualifications for the diploma fall precisely between two major requirements of American education: (1) the demand for excellence and (2) the demand for equality."[20]

Another potential problem in setting up a competency-based education program is choosing what kinds of standards to use. Competency tests exist in two general areas — those that measure school skills and those that measure life skills. The

---

[19] Quoted in *The Wall Street Journal*, May 9, 1978.
[20] National Association of Secondary School Principals, "Competency Tests and Graduation Requirements," 1976, p. 18.

Samples From High School Graduation Proficiency Tests

--- **Mathematics** ---

1. If a die (one dice) is thrown, the chance of getting a six is:

a. about even
b. less than even
c. more than even
d. none of the above

2. If a student received the following scores on tests: 85, 92, 87, 64, and 96, what was the average score?

a. 78.5
b. 84.8
c. 85.8
d. none of the above

--- **Reading** ---

3. Read this statement:

Women should have the right to be educated to their full potential along with men.

If a person expressed this view, which ideas below would he or she most likely believe?

1. A woman's place is in the home.
2. Women should refuse to do any housework.
3. If women do the same work as men, they should receive equal pay.
4. Women should make all of the important world decisions.
5. Women and men should share household tasks.
6. It was a mistake to give women the right to vote.

    a. numbers 1 and 6
    b. numbers 2 and 4
    c. numbers 3 and 5
    d. numbers 4 and 5

4. Read the following paragraph carefully.

All the students in Leslie's ninth-grade class took a trip to Chicago. A special bus was chartered for the trip. They visited the Aquarium, the Planetarium, and the Lincoln Park Zoo. At lunch time, the thirty-two ninth graders filed into the cafeteria at Marshall Field's. What a lot of hamburgers were consumed!

After reading the paragraph above, which of the following statements could you correctly assume?

    a. Leslie took a trip to Chicago.
    b. The Planetarium was the most enjoyable part of the trip.
    c. The bus driver was nervous about driving thirty-two ninth graders.
    d. They all ate lunch at one o'clock.

ANSWERS: 1-B; 2-B; 3-C; 4-A

Source: National Association of Secondary School Principals.

former require mastering techniques for school, such as multiplication tables and verb conjugations. The latter require learning skills used outside the classroom, like balancing a checkbook or following instructions on a driver's license examination. A third kind of minimal competency test — the basic skills test — examines skills used both in and out of school, such as reading, writing and arithmetic.

After determining the general type of test to use, a school board must then decide on the format — whether to use a written or oral test, or some other type of test that involves demonstrating an ability, such as making correct change in purchasing an item. Schools must also determine in which grades the tests should be administered and what type of remediation program, if any, to set up. Moreover, there are the questions of how many minimal competencies to test and how high to set the minimal standards. Some states allow individual school districts to set the lowest acceptable scores and base them on considerations such as community characteristics, faculty composition and school spending. Other jurisdictions have adopted graduated standards, based on individual ability rather than on a single standard. Using extremely low minimum standards can bring charges that the tests are meaningless. Yet, according to the Education Commission of the States, most state high school graduate competency tests are set at the eighth-grade level or below.

Dropping Tests as Diploma Requirement

The minimal-competency movement has reached the point where most of the states have initiated some sort of pupil-performance evaluation programs. There is some evidence, though, of a shift away from standardized tests for high school graduation. "Things are slowing down at the policy level, but they are speeding up at the local, district and state levels," Chris Pipho of the Education Commission of the States told Editorial Research Reports. "The concept of minimum standards in some fashion will stay around. There is a trend to make it more of an early warning system rather than to use it for high school graduation standards." Pipho pointed out that several state legislatures this year passed laws that emphasized yearly testing and remediation rather than mandatory completion of competency tests for high school graduation.

The Massachusetts State Board of Education in June 1978 set standards for basic competency skills of mathematics and communications that take effect in September 1980 at the lower elementary, upper elementary and secondary school levels. But the board stressed that its purpose was "not to establish a new condition for promotion or graduation" but rather to "improve

The British Problem

Complaints about the quality of education are not confined to America. The Times of London assailed the British education system in an editorial last March for "turning out too many children grossly ill-equipped for the everyday needs of adult life." The newspaper was disturbed particularly about the inability of young Britons to solve simple math problems. Two-thirds of a group of 15-year-old Londoners could not add up the weekly cost of buying two bottles of milk a day at 25 cents apiece.

The British math problem is being attributed to the teaching of the "new math" in place of the old rote learning. Many students emerge from school with a rudimentary knowledge of binary numbers but without the basic skills necessary to balance a checkbook.

basic skills competency in partnership with local school officials."[21] Massachusetts school districts have the option of using a state-prepared test, a commercial test approved by the State Department of Education, or a locally drawn-up test approved by the department. Similar programs that do not involve standards for graduation or grade promotion have been approved in Louisiana, Michigan, Missouri, Nebraska, New Hampshire, New Mexico, Rhode Island and Washington.

Support for competency tests for high school graduation is by no means waning. New York State recently adopted new student tests in writing and mathematics that will be used as requirements for high school graduation beginning in June 1981. *The New York Times* on July 30 called the tests "probably the toughest minimum-competency tests in the country." This action by the New York State Board of Regents shows that the movement is still strong in spite of the controversy it has spawned and the opposition it has aroused in many teachers' groups.

One reason for the movement's strength may be the praise it has received from many state educators. Ralph D. Turlington, the Florida commissioner of education, has said that the Florida program of minimal competency tests is "the most important improvement in education that we have ever undertaken." Turlington said the "biggest single impact has been attitudinal. It has encouraged people to become more serious about education. Students are working harder, and the overall result has been more financial support for education."[22] If state education officials continue to express satisfaction with minimal competency tests, there is little doubt that they will soon become an integral part of American public education.

---

[21] Quoted by Chris Pipho, "State Activity: Minimal Competency Testing," Education Commission of the States, July 10, 1978, p. 6.

[22] Quoted in *The New York Times,* July 24, 1978.

Books

Armbruster, Frank E., *Our Children's Crippled Future: How American Education Has Failed,* Quadrangle, 1977.
Flesch, Rudolf, *Why Johnny Can't Read,* Harper & Row, 1955.
Hoffmann, Banesh, *The Tyranny of Testing,* Crowell-Collier, 1962.
Kline, Morris, *Why Johnny Can't Add,* St. Martin's, 1973
Silberman, Charles, *Crisis in the Classroom,* Random House, 1970.

Articles

Gest, Kathryn Waters, "Educational Competency Standards Being Pushed," *Congressional Quarterly Weekly Report,* Oct. 15, 1977.
Hershman, Arlene, "Stretching School Dollars," *Dun's Review,* June 1978.
"High Schools Under Fire," *Time,* Nov. 14, 1977.
Pipho, Chris, "Minimal Competency Testing: A Look at State Standards," *Education Leadership,* April 1977.
Today's Education, selected issues.

Reports and Studies

College Entrance Examination Board, "On Further Examination: Report of the Advisory Panel on the Scholastic Aptitude Test Score Decline," 1977.
Editorial Research Reports, "Education's Return to Basics," 1975 Vol. II, p. 667; "Educational Equality," 1973 Vol. II, p. 645; "Reform of Public Schools," 1970 Vol. I, p. 279; "Educational Testing," 1958 Vol. II, p. 935.
Gadway, Charles J., "Functional Literacy: Basic Reading Performance," The National Right to Read Effort, 1976.
Miller, Barbara Soloth, ed., "Minimum Competency Testing: A Report of Four Regional Conferences," Education Commission of the States, January 1978.
National Academy of Education, "Improving Educational Achievement: Report of the National Academy Education Commission on Testing and Basic Skills," 1978.
National Assessment of Educational Progress, "Analysis of Supplemental Background Questions on Homework and TV," April 9, 1978.
——"Changes in Political Knowledge and Attitudes, 1969-76," Feb. 2, 1978.
——"Reading in America: A Perspective in Two Assessments," October 1976.
National Association of Secondary School Principals, "Guidelines for Improving SAT Scores," 1978.
——"Competency Tests and Graduation Requirements," 1976.
National Education Association, "The Florida Accountability Program: An Evaluation of its Educational Soundness and Implementation," July 1978.
Pipho, Chris, "State Activity: Minimal Competency Testing," Education Commission of the States, July 10, 1978.

SEX EDUCATION

by

Marc Leepson

Aug. 28
1 9 8 1

SEX EDUCATION

SEX EDUCATION is one of the most controversial issues in American public education. Recent opinion polls indicate that a large majority of Americans approve of teaching sex education in public schools.[1] Yet such courses are mandatory only in New Jersey, Maryland and the District of Columbia. Even when sex education is provided in schools, birth control often is not discussed. Experts estimate that fewer than one-third of all U.S. public-school students are taking sex education courses that include instruction in contraception.

Unlike most school subjects, sex education deals with a sensitive, highly personal area of life — one that some parents believe should not be discussed in the classroom. These parents maintain that it is their responsibility — or that of their priest, minister or rabbi — to instruct their sons and daughters on sexual matters. Most opponents of sex education see nothing wrong with schools providing instruction in human biology and the "facts of life." What they object to is what they say are the unintended messages of many sex education programs: to encourage children to experiment with sex and to disregard traditional and religious moral teachings.

Sex education programs "constitute not instruction but indoctrination," said Jacqueline Kasun, a professor of economics at Humboldt State University and an opponent of sex education in schools. These programs teach "that any kind of sexual choice is perfectly all right and is up to the individual, provided only that it does not produce babies. And that includes homosexuality. It includes masturbation. It includes sex outside of marriage."[2]

Opposition to sex education is not limited to religious fundamentalists. Psychoanalyst and educator Bruno Bettelheim, for example, believes there is little that teachers can do to influence teen-agers in sexual matters. "In my opinion, sex education is impossible in a classroom," he said recently. "Sex

---

[1] A national survey conducted in May 1981 for *Time* magazine by the research firm of Yankelovich, Skelly and White found that 70 percent of those polled approved of sex education classes in public schools that included information on birth control; 25 percent disapproved. In a Gallup Poll released Jan. 23, 1978, 77 percent of those questioned said they thought sex education should be taught in schools and 69 percent said sex education courses should include instruction in contraception.

[2] Quoted in *U.S. News & World Report*, Oct. 6, 1980, p. 89.

education is a continuous process, and it begins the moment you are born. It's in how you are bathed, how you are diapered, how you are toilet-trained, in respect for the body, in the notion that bodily feelings are pleasant and that bodily functions are not disgusting. . . . How you feel about sex comes from watching how your parents live together, how they enjoy each other's company, the respect they have for each other. . . . The problem in sex is sexual anxiety, and you cannot teach about sexual anxiety because each person has different anxieties."[3]

Scott Thompson, executive director of the National Association of Secondary School Principals, agrees with Bettelheim. Thompson believes sex education will not help decrease the number of teen-age pregnancies nor cut back on the spread of venereal disease among young persons because these are "matters of attitudes and values and outlooks." "Most high school people have been so well inoculated with the attitudes and values of films, publications, rock music and television programs . . . ," Thompson said in a recent interview, "that by the time they are 14 or 15 years old, any attempt on the part of the schools to counsel caution . . . or even to teach something in the way of birth control, is really not going to be that effective or have that much impact on what happens. . . ."[4]

Thompson maintains that sex education in secondary schools is a waste of money. "We shouldn't be throwing our money away on these kinds of efforts," he said, "because they are not going to have any impact. Let's spend our money on things that schools can teach like writing and reading, music and art. We can do that. We can't teach kids not to play around — given the society that we're in."

Arguments in Favor of Sex Education

Those in favor of sex education classes in public schools say that it provides young people with knowledge that could help bring down the alarming rate of teen-age pregnancy *(see p. 186)*. "If nothing else, just by giving young people a better notion of the risk of pregnancy that's involved and giving them accurate information and referral to services where they can get contraception, sex education certainly ought to do something to keep down the pregnancy rate," Richard Lincoln, senior vice president of the Alan Guttmacher Institute, told Editorial Research Reports.[5]

Peter Scales, director of the National Study on Barriers to Sex Education, contends that the goals of sex education go

---

[3] Interview with Elizabeth Hall in *Psychology Today,* July 1981, p. 40.
[4] The National Association of Secondary School Principals is located in Reston, Va.
[5] The Alan Guttmacher Institute, a research and analysis corporation, is affiliated with Planned Parenthood.

Sex education deals with a sensitive, highly personal area of life.

beyond helping avoid unwanted pregnancies and venereal disease. "Sex education should be approached not as a solution to a problem, but as a natural response to an irrefutable need," he said. "It provides young people with the skills to make choices in a world that is far more socially complex than the one their parents had to deal with."[6] Scales believes that religious training and parental information about sex often are inadequate. "It's fine and good when young people find firm guidance in religious teachings and in what parents have told them," he said, "but communication between parents and their children on sexual matters is typically characterized by evasiveness and embarrassed silence. Also, kids these days don't get all their values and information from parents and church, if they ever did. They get them from television, from records, from their friends, from public school bathrooms — you name it."

Some of those who support sex education generally believe that the subject is not suited for every school. "Sex education is appropriate in schools where morale is high, where students are enthusiastic and involved. In such an emotionally reinforcing environment, schools may be able to help adolescents develop a better awareness of their own sexuality as well as a greater sensitivity to others," wrote Syracuse University Professor Sol Gordon. "But in schools where morale is low and students are generally apathetic, it is doubtful that a course in sex education can have a positive influence. . . . Among students who are gen-

---

[6] Quoted in *U.S. News & World Report*, Oct. 6, 1980, p. 89.

erally apathetic and clearly 'turned off,' traditional sex education designed to influence attitudes and sexual behavior is not
likely to produce significant results."[7]

Different State Policies on the Issue

According to a Gallup Poll released Oct. 4, 1978, about 43
percent of students aged 13-18 reported having had any sex
education in school. But only 31 percent of that group said they
were taught about contraception. A 1979 study conducted by
Professor Melvin Zelnik of Johns Hopkins University[8] indicated
that two-thirds of female students aged 15-19 had some sex
education courses in school; less than half said they had instruction in birth control methods. Ninety percent of those girls who
received sex education said their courses included information
about venereal disease; nearly all were taught about the men-
strual cycle.

Maryland, New Jersey and the District of Columbia are the
only jurisdictions that require local school boards to provide sex
education instruction. Kentucky has a law requiring that sex
education be offered as part of mandatory health classes but has
no specific policy as to how the program should be implemented. Six states — Delaware, Iowa, Kansas, Minnesota,
Pennsylvania and Utah — encourage, but do not mandate, local
school districts to offer sex education courses. Twenty-two
states leave the decision to the local school boards; the remaining 19 states have no official policy on the matter *(see map, p.
183)*. Michigan and Louisiana at one time had laws banning the
teaching of sex education in schools. The Michigan law was
repealed in 1977, the Louisiana law in 1979.

The New Jersey Board of Education in August 1980 ordered
all of the state's school districts to set up sex education courses
— called "family life" courses — by September 1983. The
courses are to begin no later than the sixth grade and continue
through high school. Local school districts will be permitted to
draw up their schools' courses. Students may be excused from
the classes if their parents wish. The school board's action
spawned a debate in the New Jersey legislature. Among the
groups lobbying against the order were the State Teachers
Association, the State School Boards Association and the New
Jersey Right to Life Committee. Among those favoring the
measure were Planned Parenthood, the Junior League and the
Roman Catholic Church.

The state teachers and school board associations opposed the

---

[7] Sol Gordon, *et al., The Sexual Adolescent* (1979), pp. 49-50.
[8] Melvin Zelnik, "Sex Education and Knowledge of Pregnancy Risk Among U.S. Teenage
Women," *Family Planning Perspectives*, Vol. XII, 1980.

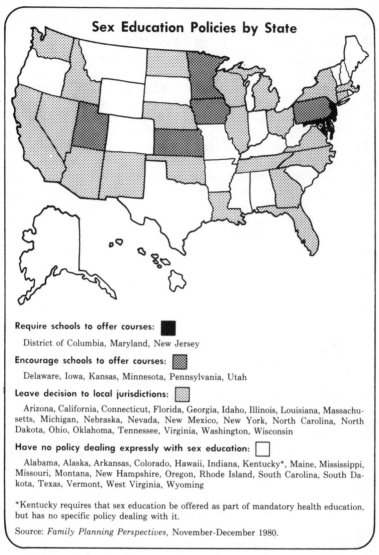

Sex Education Policies by State

Require schools to offer courses: ■

District of Columbia, Maryland, New Jersey

Encourage schools to offer courses: ▨

Delaware, Iowa, Kansas, Minnesota, Pennsylvania, Utah

Leave decision to local jurisdictions: ▨

Arizona, California, Connecticut, Florida, Georgia, Idaho, Illinois, Louisiana, Massachusetts, Michigan, Nebraska, Nevada, New Mexico, New York, North Carolina, North Dakota, Ohio, Oklahoma, Tennessee, Virginia, Washington, Wisconsin

Have no policy dealing expressly with sex education: □

Alabama, Alaska, Arkansas, Colorado, Hawaii, Indiana, Kentucky*, Maine, Mississippi, Missouri, Montana, New Hampshire, Oregon, Rhode Island, South Carolina, South Dakota, Texas, Vermont, West Virginia, Wyoming

*Kentucky requires that sex education be offered as part of mandatory health education, but has no specific policy dealing with it.

Source: *Family Planning Perspectives*, November-December 1980.

plan primarily because they felt sex education was an issue that should be handled solely by local school boards. Others opposed the plan because they did not believe sex education should be taught in public schools. The state's Right to Life Committee objected to the program because the school board's guidelines allowed abortion to be taught as an alternative to childbirth. The New Jersey Assembly on June 11 turned back an attempt to overturn the school board order when it voted down a bill that would have prohibited any state agency from ordering local school boards to have sex education programs. Opponents of sex education say they will continue to challenge the ruling in the coming months.

Local School Boards' Varying Approaches

In Virginia, one of the 22 states that leaves the decision on setting up sex education programs to local school districts, two school boards in the Washington, D.C., area voted this year to broaden existing sex education programs. The Fairfax County School Board's May 14 vote to liberalize its high school sex education program ended a five-year debate on the subject. Thousands of parents had objected to changing the existing sex education plan. A petition opposing the change was signed by 10,000 persons and presented to the school board. But the board voted 8-2 to overturn a ban on teaching what had been termed the "big five": contraception, abortion, masturbation, homosexuality and rape. The board also voted to allow parents to remove their children from the new course and instead take one of two alternative courses on human anatomy and reproduction.

"The sex education course was something totally new. . . . Trying to express my views was hard and frustrating at times. My values, which I had thought were solid and ironclad, turned out to be unsure, and often contradicted one another. It was great trying to understand myself through myself."

Massachusetts high school senior (female)

Among those lobbying against broadening the sex education program in Fairfax County was a group called the Northern Virginia Movement to Restore Decency. Elizabeth Burch, a representative of the group, said she was "absolutely horrified" at the school board's decision. "There are no values being taught there," she said. "Students won't know what's right or wrong. It's not right to have premarital sex. It's not right to have an abortion. The Ten Commandments should be their standards."[9] The school board's action came after a survey indicated that 75 percent of the county's parents favored expanding the sex education program in the schools.

On June 24 the Alexandria, Va., school board voted unanimously to direct the county's school staff to begin working on a curriculum for sex education courses. The new courses, which will begin in September 1982, will cover not only the "big five," but also child rearing, the integrity of the family, divorce and making "responsible choices" about sex. Contrary to the experience in neighboring Fairfax County, the Alexandria school

---

[9] Quoted in *The Washington Post*, May 15, 1981.

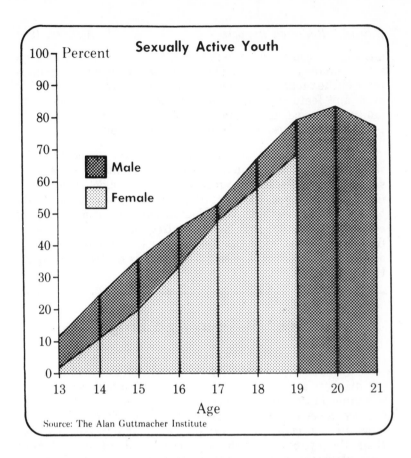

Percent **Sexually Active Youth**

Source: The Alan Guttmacher Institute

board's action came without acrimonious debate. The main reason, officials said, was that the school board worked closely with parent groups in studying the issue and formulating the basis for the new program.

Education experts point to sex education programs in Flint, Mich., and Falls Church, Va., as among the most successful in the nation. The Flint Family Life Education Program begins in grade four, when students study the facts of reproduction. In grades 10-12, the program concentrates on "psycho-social and psycho-sexual concepts." The entire program tries to help students develop a system of values to help them with decisions about sex. It encourages participation by parents, including instruction to help parents communicate with their children on sexual matters.

The Falls Church program also involves parents. Among other things, the school system sponsors seminars for parents in which they learn the program's details. The program — which is optional for students — consists of a year-long Life Sciences course for sixth graders, another course for ninth graders and a

185

one-quarter course called Seminar on Human Sexuality for high
school juniors and seniors. The sixth-grade course is the center-
piece of the program. It teaches human anatomy, the human life
cycle and features no-questions-barred discussions about sexuality. The goal, as in the Flint, Mich., program, is to help
teenagers make responsible decisions about sex.

"The kids are exposed to so much aberrant sexual behavior
that sex education counteracts this media blitz we're seeing,"
said Mary Lee Tatum, who teaches the high school senior seminar in Falls Church. "The course gives the kids an opportunity
to talk about something more than the fantasy images they see
constantly." Tatum said the most frequently asked question
from students is, "How can I get him or her to like me?" They
are curious about sex, she said, "but that is far from the major
topic of interest."[10]

Problem of Teen-Age Pregnancy

A dvocates and opponents of sex education have at least one
thing in common: concern about the alarmingly high incidence of teen-age pregnancy in the United States. The problems are especially acute for pregnant, unmarried girls. For
them, the joys of childbirth often become a depressing future of
unemployment, poverty, welfare dependency, emotional stress
and health problems for mother and child.[11] For married teen-
agers — both mother and father — the birth of a child abruptly
signals the end of youth and the beginning of adult responsibilities, an experience described by rock musician Bruce
Springsteen:

> Then I got Mary pregnant
> And, man, that was all she wrote
> And for my 19th birthday I got a union card
>   and a wedding coat
> We went down to the courthouse
> And the judge put it all to rest
> No wedding day smiles, no walk down the aisle,
> No flowers, no wedding dress
>
> — "The River," © 1979-80 by Bruce Springsteen,
>   used by permission

In 1978, the last year for which complete statistics are available, some 1.1 million girls aged 15-19 became pregnant; about

---

[10] Quoted in *The Washington Post,* April 4, 1981.
[11] See "Teen-age Pregnancy," *E.R.R.,* 1979 Vol. I, pp. 205-224.

540,000 actually gave birth. Of those births, 44.9 percent were out of wedlock. Some 29,500 girls below age 15 became pregnant in 1978; about 10,800 gave birth. More than one teen-age girl in 10 gets pregnant each year and, according to the Alan Guttmacher Institute, if patterns do not change, four in 10 of the girls who turned 14 in 1981 will have at least one pregnancy while still in their teens; two in 10 will give birth at least once. Some 1.3 million children now live with teen-age mothers — half of whom are unmarried. An additional 1.6 million children under age five live with mothers who were teen-agers when they gave birth.[12]

Those on both sides of the sex education debate also are concerned about the high rate of venereal disease among teen-agers. According to the federal Center for Disease Control, the incidence of gonorrhea — the No. 1 reportable communicable disease in the United States — is nearly three times higher among teen-agers than among the general population. In 1979, the last year for which complete statistics are available, the gonorrhea rate for boys and girls aged 15-19 was 1,211.4 per 100,000 population, compared to the general population rate of 459.4. The rate of primary and secondary syphilis for teen-agers was 16.2 per 100,000 population; for all ages the rate was 11.4 *(see box, p. 190)*. These figures represent reported VD cases, but medical authorities say that hundreds of thousands of cases of gonorrhea and syphilis go unreported each year.[13]

Questions About Value of Sex Education

While it is argued that teen-age pregnancy and venereal disease are serious problems, there is no agreement on what to do about them. Most sex education advocates say that the best way to prevent teen-age pregnancy and venereal disease is to provide pertinent information in sex education classes. Sex education proponents also advocate providing social services to unwed teen-agers through government-financed family planning centers.

Opponents of sex education, on the other hand, say that teaching about sex in schools and helping teen-agers with birth control and family planning are not only the wrong answers to the problem, but, in fact, contribute to the problem. Connaught Marshner, president of the Pro-Family Coalition, an organization that represents some 100 state and local family-oriented groups, says that sex education proponents ignore the "root cause of the escalation of teen-age pregnancy, which is promiscuity." Marshner believes that sex education courses and family

[12] Statistics from the Alan Guttmacher Institute, "Teenage Pregnancy: The Problem That Hasn't Gone Away," March 1981.
[13] See "Venereal Disease: Continuing Problem," *E.R.R.,* 1979 Vol. I, pp. 45-64.

planning centers foster "indiscriminate sex" among teen-agers. Why are teen-agers having indiscriminate sex? "Because they have been cultivated in a mindset, in a mentality, that anything goes," Marshner said, "and that abstinence is not an acceptable alternative, and this is the promiscuity mindset."[14]

Those favoring sex education say that it has not been proven that such instruction puts "ideas" in teen-agers' heads. "There has been no evidence that sex education has had any effect on sexual activity," Richard Lincoln of the Alan Guttmacher Institute told Editorial Research Reports. "The few studies that there have been have shown that it has no effect. It hasn't increased it; hasn't decreased it. There has not been a national study of the subject so there's no way of definitely answering that question." Lincoln added: "Theoretically, I would think that a better informed young person is better able to resist exploitative sex and to make more rational decisions about sexual activity and resist the pressures than one who is poorly informed. But I think ... it [sex education] probably has very little effect on sexual activity."

Debate in Congress on Family Planning

The argument over the merits of sex education parallels the recent debate in Congress on the future of the only federal government agency that provides family planning services, the Office for Family Planning in the Department of Health and Human Services. The office provides funds that help finance some 5,100 family planning counseling centers throughout the country and another 27 centers that focus primarily on pregnant teen-agers and parents under age 18. Congress set up the larger program a decade ago under Title X of the Public Health Services Act of 1970. The counseling centers, which provided services to some 4 million women last year, give physical examinations and birth control advice that includes referral service for abortion. The teen-age counseling program was begun three years ago to try to deal with the rising numbers of teen-age pregnancies. In the current fiscal year family planning will receive some $162 million in federal funds.

The first salvo in the war of words over the government's role in family planning and sex education came Jan. 29 when Health and Human Services Secretary Richard S. Schweiker told a news conference in Washington, D.C., that he believed sex education was primarily a responsibility of parents. "I don't think it's the fed's role to do it," he said, "and I don't think it's the state's role unless the local school agency does it with the express approval of the parent." Schweiker later explained to the House Ways and Means Committee that he did not want to

---

[14] Appearing on "The MacNeil/Lehrer Report," PBS-TV, June 23, 1981.

do away with governmental family planning support but that he was against having the government directly involved. "I support family planning per se," he told the panel Feb. 25. "The point I was trying to make was I didn't think the government should completely supplant the family in this operation and push them aside."

A congressional challenge to the teen-age family planning centers came this year from freshman Sen. Jeremiah Denton, R-Ala., who sponsored a bill that as originally drafted called for the promotion of teen-age "chastity" as a solution to "the problem of adolescent promiscuity." The bill originally defined "promiscuity" as "having sexual intercourse out of wedlock," but that language was left out of the final version, approved by the Senate Labor and Human Resources Committee June 24 and ultimately accepted by a House-Senate conference committee July 28.

"I have positive and negative feelings about the sex education course I took in high school. It was difficult to discuss sex in the open.... But looking back on it, I think it was more valuable than I thought at the time.... Many of the things I learned there I would not have learned at all or would have been learned from sources that wouldn't have been accurate."

New Jersey college senior (male)

Denton's measure provides federal funds for family planning but with the goal of promoting "self-discipline" among teen-agers. It continues funding the 27 centers that aid pregnant adolescents but also funds an as-yet-unspecified number of other educational centers designed to reach teen-agers before they become sexually active. The aim, an aide to Sen. Denton said, is to encourage teen-agers that "it is OK to say 'no.' "[15] Denton's bill was accepted by House and Senate conferees over the vehement objections of Rep. Toby Moffett, D-Conn., who called the new organizations "store-front chastity centers." Moffett said: "We're going to be laughed out of every junior high school in America for being irrelevant."

At the July 28 House-Senate reconciliation conference that discussed the measure, Moffett asked why Denton and other conservatives wanted to get the government into the business of counseling on sexual mores. Denton responded: "We are now teaching them to say 'yes' with government money. This bill is

---

[15] See Congressional Quarterly's *Weekly Report*, Aug. 1, 1981, p. 1388.

Teen-Age Venereal Disease Rates*

Gonorrhea

Year	Boys, Ages 10-14	Girls, Ages 10-14	Total, Ages 10-14	Boys, Ages 15-19	Girls, Ages 15-19	Total, Ages 15-19
1979	22.2	79.7	50.4	956.6	1,468.8	1,211.4
1978	22.8	76.8	49.3	977.6	1,481.7	1,228.9
1975	21.1	74.4	47.2	1,121.5	1,462.4	1,292.2
1969	17.5	25.7	21.5	895.8	532.4	712.5

Syphilis**

Year	Boys, Ages 10-14	Girls, Ages 10-14	Total, Ages 10-14	Boys, Ages 15-19	Girls, Ages 15-19	Total, Ages 15-19
1979	.4	1.2	.8	18.0	14.4	16.2
1978	.6	1.0	.8	16.5	12.7	14.6
1975	.7	1.5	1.1	18.3	17.7	18.0
1969	.7	1.4	1.1	18.1	19.7	18.9

*Per 100,000 population
**Primary and secondary syphilis.
Source: Center for Disease Control

intended to offer an alternative organizational setup." Denton and cosponsor Sen. Orrin G. Hatch, R-Utah, were supported by anti-abortion groups that are unhappy with the federal involvement in family planning.

Congress wound up authorizing the adolescent program at $30 million for each of the next three years. Of the money appropriated, one-third can be spent on "scientific research on the causes and consequences of premarital adolescent sexual relations and pregnancy." Of the remaining funds, two-thirds, or up to $13.3 million, can be spent on continuing the existing counseling center program to provide prenatal care and nutrition counseling to pregnant teen-agers. The final portion of the funding, up to $6.6 million, will go to prevention services, which will be provided by maternity homes, YWCAs and others who now operate programs for pregnant teen-agers, or by charitable or religious organizations not now involved.

The bill, as originally drafted by Sen. Denton, prohibited any reference to abortion during counseling sessions funded under the program. But the reconciliation conferees modified that restriction so information about abortion now will be provided if a teen-ager and her parents request it. The new program's primary thrust will be to promote adoption as a "positive option" for pregnant teen-agers. In order to receive counseling under the program, a teen-ager will have to have parental consent, although such permission will not be needed for testing for pregnancy or venereal disease. Counseling about contraception will continue to be allowed. Actual services, such as the provision of contraceptive devices, though, will be authorized only if not available in the community. Finally, parental permission will not be required in the current program, which also allows discussion of abortion as one of many options for pregnant teen-agers and provides contraceptive services.

One reason liberal members of Congress agreed to Denton's proposal was a compromise with conservatives over the issue of how to fund the larger 5,100-center family planning program. Conservatives, led by Sen. Hatch, had pushed to give the states responsibility for distributing funds as part of block grants authorized by Congress. That move, liberals said, would have effectively killed the program because many states would have used the money to fund other, less controversial programs. In agreement for passage of the Denton bill, Hatch and other conservatives dropped the proposal to put the Title X funds under the state block grant program.

Impact of 'Secular Humanism'

THE CONTROVERSY over sex education is being played out against the backdrop of a larger debate over the issue of secular humanism. In recent years fundamentalist Christian leaders such as the Rev. Jerry Falwell of the Moral Majority have led a campaign against secular humanism, which they characterize as an anti-Christian, anti-family ideology that has spread throughout American society. "Secular humanism has become the religion of America," Falwell said. It has "taken the place of the Bible."[16] Anti-humanists see sex education as incorporating the worst of humanism's tenets. Falwell, whose headquarters is in Lynchburg, Va., has described sex education as "academic pornography."

In its simplest form, humanism is a philosophy centered on human interests and values in which humans and their capabilities are the central concerns. "Man is the measure of all things," said Protagoras, a fifth century B.C. Greek philosopher, who historians believe first asserted the humanist position. Modern humanism has evolved through a broken and diverse route from the Renaissance, when humanism was a literary and intellectual movement concerned with ancient Greek and Roman classical studies — the humanities. "Gradually the old classical conception of man as an autonomous, independent, rational human being began to be revived," wrote historian W. Y. Jones of

---

[16] Quoted in *Newsweek*, July 6, 1981, p. 48. See also James David Besser, "Anti-Humanism on the Air," *The New Republic*, July 25, 1981, pp. 22-23.

Renaissance humanism. "That long forgotten appreciation of the value and dignity of the human personality ... so long buried under the weight of Christian humility and other-worldliness, now re-emerged."[17]

Today the term "secular humanism" has been coined to describe the philosophy of a group of people, mainly writers, scholars and educators, who reject supernatural religious beliefs and emphasize science and reason. A "Secular Humanist Declaration" issued last year by 61 humanists declared: "Men and women are free and are responsible for their own destinies and ... they cannot look toward some transcendental being for salvation." The American Humanist Association and the Ethical Culture Society (the two main humanist groups) have an estimated 10,000 members.

Link Between Humanism and Sex Education

Opponents of secular humanism say that one of the ways in which that philosophy is spread is through sex education courses. Syndicated columnist Joseph Sobran is among those who share this view. "Liberal sex education" automatically includes a "certain set of values [that is] more or less covertly superordinated over the traditional ones," he wrote. These values include the belief that "casual sex is not only permissible, it is virtually imperative." Sobran believes that sex education should be undertaken by parents and religious teachers and that sex education courses in schools constitute a usurpation of the parents' rightful role.[18]

Scott Thompson of the National Association of Secondary School Principals also believes that sex education instruction wrongfully takes over family responsibilities. "Any policy that allows my daughter, for example, to have an abortion without my knowledge I'm firmly against because I think it erodes the family," Thompson said in a recent interview. "Any policy that allows a minor to make any decision along these lines without the information of the family certainly undercuts the family and destroys the family relationship. I am very much opposed to that kind of interference in family relationships by volunteer organizations or the state."

Other opponents of sex education and secular humanism are even more outspoken. Humanists are "promoting sexual perversion," declared pastor Lee Wine of Ashland, Ore., in an Aug. 21, 1980, radio broadcast over station KDOV-AM. They are doing this because "they want to create such an obsession with sex

---

[17] W. Y. Jones, *A History of Western Philosophy* (1955), p. 57. See also "The New Humanism," *E.R.R.*, 1970 Vol. II, pp. 813-832.
[18] Writing in *The Human Life Review*, winter 1981, pp. 97, 98.

among our young people that they will have no time for interest in spiritual pursuits. . . . So what do we have? Humanist obsessions: sex, pornography, marijuana, drugs, self-indulgence, rights without responsibility."

Groups Monitoring TV Shows and Books

In addition to their fight against sex education, the anti-humanists have been active in other related areas. For example, a television watchdog group in Tupelo, Miss., the National Federation for Decency, recently announced plans to monitor "The Phil Donohue Show," an award-winning television talk show, because the group claims the program concentrates too much on sex. "Never before in television history have we had a sex activist broadcaster such as Phil Donohue," the organization said in a press release issued Aug. 1. "Approximately two out of three of his shows are sex shows, and most of these promote abnormal sex, which Mr. Donohue prefers to call 'sexual alternatives.' Such shows have a mind-warping effect on youth and adults."

Anti-humanist groups also are challenging library books, textbooks and courses of study they consider anti-family, anti-American and anti-religion. In the libraries, the focus is on material that influences children to adopt immoral or secular humanistic attitudes. This is nothing new. Parents have been objecting to what they consider too much emphasis on non-traditional values for years.[19] But what is new is the extent of today's protests.

The American Library Association reported in December 1980 that there seemed to be an unprecedented number of complaints about books in public libraries following last year's presidential election. "In the past three or four years we have had an average of three to five complaints a week," said spokesman Judith Krug. "We are now averaging three to five complaints daily."[20] The association and two other groups — the Association for Supervision and Curriculum Development and the American Association of Publishers — conducted a survey before the election and found there was a large increase in the number of complaints received by libraries and schools in 1978-1980 compared to 1976-1978.

The survey, which was released July 31, found that about 75

---

[19] In 1974, for example, violent protests erupted in Kanawha County, W.Va., over the use of new textbooks that many parents regarded as anti-American, blasphemous, critical of parental authority, immoral and obscene. As a result of the controversy, the Kanawha school system placed parents on textbook selection committees and adopted special selection guidelines. During the 1970s, parental disputes with schools also arose in Hanover County, N.C., Baton Rouge, La., and in other parts of the country. See "Education's Return to Basics," *E.R.R.*, 1975 Vol. II, pp. 668-669.
[20] Quoted by United Press International in *The New York Times*, Dec. 11, 1980.

percent of the challenges to library and classroom materials were mounted by individual parents representing only themselves. Those who challenged material on the state level, however, tended to be members of groups. "The state challenges were much more organized," Bob Doyle of the American Library Association said in a recent interview. "It wasn't just individuals objecting to a book, but rather it was a group. Of these challenges the majority centered on concerns with regard to sex or sexuality, obscenity, objectional language and those types of things." The survey found that in more than half the challenges "books or other materials either were restricted or censorship was imposed."[21]

In addition to the many local organizations and parent groups working to keep the schools and libraries free of secular humanist materials, there is a textbook reviewing "clearinghouse" in Longview, Texas. Mel and Norma Gabler started Educational Research Analysts two years ago to advise parents on how to recognize textbooks advocating humanist teachings — including evolution, negations of Christianity and sexual freedom.

Criticism of the Anti-Humanist Movement

The anti-humanist movement has its own vehement critics who claim that humanism is being used as a scapegoat for all the ills that have beset society. "I think secular humanism is a straw man," said Paul Kurtz, a philosophy professor at the State University of New York at Buffalo, and editor of *The Humanist* magazine. "They are looking for someone to blame."[22] Dorothy Massie of the National Education Association put it this way: "It's a pervasive campaign, an epidemic and a real attack on public education. . . . It's really a witch hunt, only now the witches are humanists."[23]

Charles Krauthammer, associate editor of *The New Republic* magazine, wrote recently that secular humanism has come to be "a handy catchall to evoke all the changes of the postwar American cultural revolution: challenges to traditional sexual morality, civil and parental authority, and religious orthodoxy; to work, family, neighborhood, and church, as Ronald Reagan puts it. Ultimately, it is a reaction to a decline in religious values."[24] In essence, Krauthammer wrote, the phenomenon can be explained as "conservatives opposing secularization and calling for a religious renewal." This is not a new concept, but blaming one single group is new, Krauthammer said, and "potentially dangerous."

---

[21] The survey was entitled, "Limiting What Students Shall Read: Books and Other Learning Materials in our Schools: How They are Selected and How They are Banned."
[22] Quoted in *The New York Times*, May 17, 1981.
[23] Quoted in *Newsweek*, July 6, 1981, p. 48.
[24] Writing in *The New Republic*, July 25, 1981, p. 23.

Krauthammer believes it is illogical to blame society's declining religious values on the small number of humanists and that those opposed to humanism have taken what "otherwise would have been a shadowy struggle against a 500-year-old historical trend — secularization — [and] transformed [it] into a crusade against a militant ideology controlled by a vanguard of party activists — the humanists. . . . A generation ago the pernicious sappers of our vital spiritual juices were called 'godless Communists.' Now they are 'secular humanists.' "

How much support does the movement against secular humanism have? National polls indicate that a majority of Americans do not agree with the anti-humanists' views on sex education, abortion and other controversial social issues. Although the nation has taken a conservative turn in recent years, the shift appears to be focused more on economic than on social issues. A recent poll conducted for *Time* magazine, and published in the June 1, 1981, issue, found that Americans want less government intrusion into their lives, favor increasing military strength and worry about the permissive and immoral values reflected in the media. But the poll also indicated that a majority of Americans favor the Equal Rights Amendment, oppose making abortions illegal and want strong gun control legislation. And 70 percent of the respondents approved of sex education in public schools.

A *Washington Post*-ABC News poll released June 13, found that of those who had heard or read about the Moral Majority, 43 percent generally disapproved of the organization's positions, while 37 percent approved. On social issues, 61 percent supported the Equal Rights Amendment, 74 percent said they approved of legalized abortions in most cases, two-thirds said they believed birth control devices should be made available to teen-agers and about half said there is nothing wrong with sexual relations between unmarried partners.

The national polls may indicate disfavor with the anti-humanists' positions on social issues and sex education in schools. But this does not mean that there likely will be an increase in the number of sex education courses in public schools in the near future. As long as the option of setting up sex education is left to local school boards — as it is in 48 states — there probably will be no widespread movement to institute new and expanded courses on sex education. The main reason, analysts say, is that most local school boards are conservative in nature and highly sensitive to criticism from parents. And sex education is one issue that usually elicits strong feelings from parents nearly everywhere in the country.

Selected Bibliography

Books

Gordon, Sol, Peter Scales and Kathleen Everly, *The Sexual Adolescent: Communicating with Teenagers about Sex,* 2nd ed., Duxbury Press, 1979.

Jones, Richard M., *Fantasy and Feeling in Education,* New York University Press, 1968.

Osofsky, Howard J., *The Pregnant Teenager,* Charles C. Thomas, 1968.

Pogrebin, Letty Cottin, *Growing Up Free: Raising Your Child in the 80s,* McGraw-Hill, 1980.

Read, Donald A., Sidney B. Simon and Joel B. Goodman, *Health Education: The Search for Values,* Prentice-Hall, 1977.

Sorensen, Robert C., *Adolescent Sexuality in Contemporary America,* World, 1973.

Articles

Castleman, Michael, "Why Teenagers Get Pregnant," *The Nation,* Nov. 26, 1977.

Family Planning Perspectives, published by the Alan Guttmacher Institute, selected issues.

Horner, Constance, "Is the New Sex Education Going Too Far?" *The New York Times Magazine,* Dec. 7, 1980.

Krauthammer, Charles, "The Humanist Phantom," *The New Republic,* July 25, 1981.

"Our Children are Treated Like Idiots," interview with Bruno Bettelheim by Elizabeth Hall, *Psychology Today,* July 1981.

Pelman, Ann, "Conferees Vote Teen-Age Chastity Program," *Congressional Quarterly Weekly Report,* Aug. 1, 1981.

Sobran, Joseph, "Sex Education," *The Human Life Review,* winter 1981.

Reports and Studies

Alan Guttmacher Institute, "Teenage Pregnancy: The Problem That Hasn't Gone Away," 1981.

—— "Eleven Million Teenagers," 1976.

Editorial Research Reports: "Teen-Age Pregnancy," 1979 Vol. I, p. 205; "Venereal Disease: Continuing Problem," 1979 Vol. I, p. 45; "Sexual Revolution: Myth or Reality," 1970 Vol. I, p. 241; "The New Humanism," 1970 Vol. II, p. 813.

U.S. Center for Disease Control, "An Analysis of U.S. Sex Education Programs and Evaluation," July 1979.

INDEX